THE KIDDS OF KING & QUEEN COUNTY, VIRGINIA, 1691-1855

Compiled by Reiley Kidd, MD
and Sandra K. Kidd
© October 2020

Published by Lulu.com, Morrisville, North Carolina USA

The Kidds of King and Queen County, Virginia, 1691-1855

Compiled by:

Reiley Kidd, MD, of Seattle, WA and

Sandra K. Kidd, of Decatur, GA

We ask that you credit this book or our website www.kiddroots.org when using this
information, and that you use it in its original form. Thank you.

ISBN: 978-1-71652-184-3 (paperback)

Published by Lulu.com.

TABLE OF CONTENTS

This Table of Contents lists the given names of all the individuals who appear in this compilation.

When two or more individuals share the same given name, they appear in chronological order of their appearance in the records.

INTRODUCTION

This compilation is a compendium (or inventory) of all historical records found to date that mention any individual with the surname of Kidd in King & Queen County, Virginia from 1747 (the year in which the first Kidd record was made in K&Q) through 1855.

We began the ambitious task of producing these compilations for over twenty Virginia counties with several objectives:

1. To find virtually every existing record mentioning the surname of Kidd in these Virginia counties prior to 1850;

2. To analyze these records and ascertain (if possible) whether the individuals are descendants of the Thomas Kidd who arrived in the Virginia colony by 1646, and if so, their line of descent; and

3. To distinguish between proven, documented relationships and those which are widely shared and held to be accurate, but for which proof is minimal or non-existent.

KING & QUEEN COUNTY AND ITS RECORDS

King & Queen County was formed in 1691 from New Kent County, and named in honor of King William III and Queen Mary. A long, narrow county, K&Q County is bounded by Caroline (NW), Essex (E to NE), Middlesex (SE), Gloucester (SE), King William (W to SW), and New Kent Counties (SW), as the map on the next page illustrates. Much of its southern border is delineated by the Mattaponi River.

Unfortunately for researchers, the county courthouse, along with most of its records, has burned three times – in 1828, 1833, and again in 1864, during the Civil War, making it one of Virginia's worst "burned records" counties. Birth, death and marriage records are available from 1853, and earliest land and probate records begin in 1864. K&Q Tax lists for personal property and land begin in 1782; fortunately for us, those records were stored at the state level, and have survived. **Because so few other records for K&Q have survived, these land and personal property tax lists are very valuable sources in our research and analysis.**

This compilation attempts to collate all public records from King & Queen County for individuals with the Kidd surname, organized by their given names. When more than one person shared a given name, we've attempted to subdivide those facts where possible to distinguish between the different individuals; where not possible, we've left the data elements under one name, while acknowledging that those facts may represent more than one person.

During the era covered by this compilation, King and Queen County was divided into three parishes. The parish system came from the Church of England, and the Virginia General Assembly established them and defined their boundaries. Following the Revolutionary War and the disestablishment of the Church of England as the official state church, these parish divisions were maintained, and most of the duties of the vestry (care of the poor, maintenance of the roads, biennial processioning of land boundaries) were turned over to county officials. Parish boundaries continued to be used as geographic designations in tax and other records. The parish of residence is also given on the 1850 federal census, and is useful in determining in which part of the county an individual resided. From 1723 on, **Stratton Major Parish** was the lower parish, **St. Stephens Parish** was the middle parish, and **Drysdale Parish** was the upper parish. See the Figure, below.

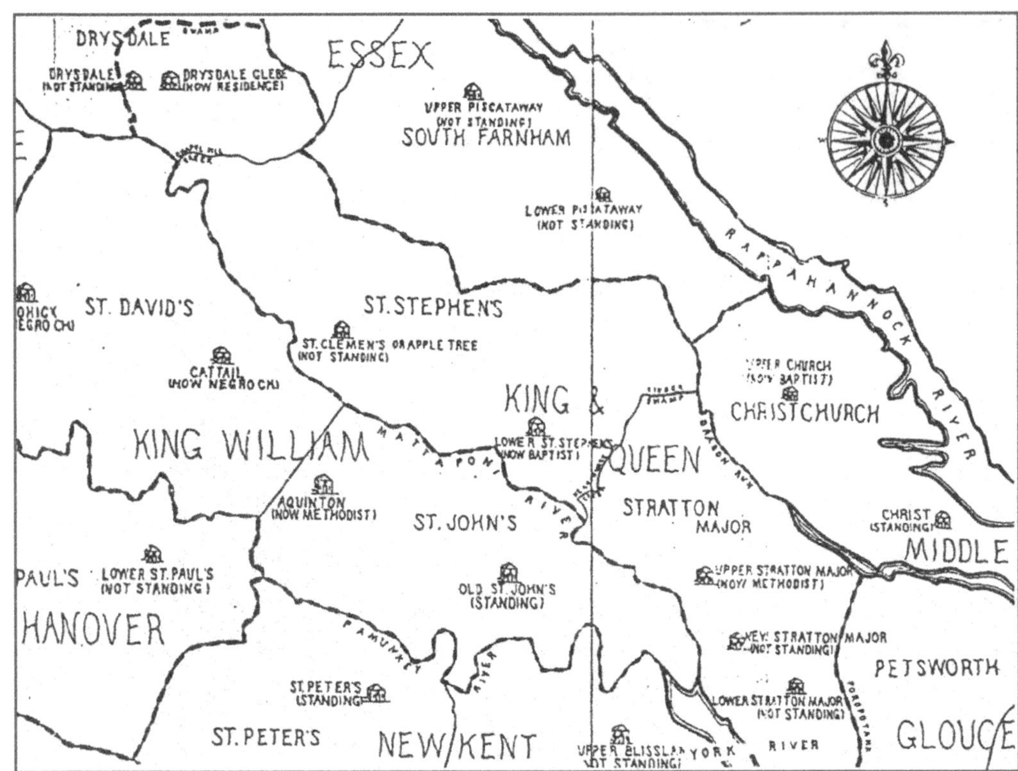

FIGURE: An outline map of the parishes of King & Queen County and its neighboring counties (Essex to the north, Middlesex and Gloucester to the south and east, King William to the south and west, and Caroline to the northwest).[1] St. Stephens (later Drysdale Parish after 1785) included parts of both Caroline and King & Queen Cos.

ORIGINS OF THE EARLY KIDDS IN KING & QUEEN COUNTY

The Kidd families found in early King & Queen County, Virginia most likely originated in neighboring Middlesex County, Virginia. **Thomas1 Kidd** was in the Virginia colony by 7 October 1646, when he was named in an estate record for Peter Deare in York County. Although we have no record of his passage to Virginia, Thomas is believed to be our immigrant ancestor.

Thomas1 Kidd and his only known wife **Jane** (whose maiden name is not confirmed or documented in any historical record) were married no later than 1669. They were the parents of **two sons: Thomas2 and William2; and three daughters: Elizabeth, Jane, and Mary**. The births of all their children except Thomas2 (who was born prior to the formation of Middlesex County) are recorded in the Middlesex Christ Church Parish Register. **Thomas1 Kidd** wrote his will 28 May 1680 and died by October 1680 at his farm in Middlesex County. Through his will, Thomas left his properties to his eldest son **Thomas2 Kidd** and Thomas2's heirs. He also left his younger son **William2 Kidd** a property that William had the right to live on during his lifetime. This practice of leaving the land to the oldest son is called primogeniture or entail, which means the property is

---

[1] From *"A Merchant's Account Book: King and Queen County, Virginia, 1750 1751,"* *Magazine of Virginia Genealogy,* 28 (February 1990): 61-65 [map on p. 63]. This article copied the map from C. G. (Churchill Gibson) Chamberlayne, *The Vestry Book of Petsworth Parish, Gloucester County, Virginia, 1677-1793.* Virginia State Library, 1933, frontispiece. The book cites the author of the map as Rev. A. LeB. Ribble of Herndon, Va.

passed on only to the eldest son of each successive generation. A custom of British law, this practice was used in the Virginia colony until abolished in the 1780s.

Thomas2 Kidd, the elder son of **Thomas1 Kidd**, likely was born by 1669 before Middlesex County was formed from Lancaster County. No parish books of Lancaster County have survived. **William2 Kidd,** the younger son of **Thomas1 Kidd**, was born 22 March 1675/1676 in Middlesex Co VA and baptized at Christ Church Parish as the son of Thomas and Jane Kidd. For the next 47 years after their father's death, Thomas and Jane's sons Thomas and William would live side by side on adjoining properties close by the Dragon Run,[2] raising their families and their crops. They likely never traveled more than 10 miles from home during their lifetimes. **Thomas2 Kidd** married **Alice Trigg**, and **William2 Kidd** married a woman named **Margaret**, whose maiden name is not confirmed or documented in any historical record.

In the spring of 1727, it is likely that some sort of disease or epidemic struck Middlesex County. It was to take the lives of **William2 Kidd**, his wife Margaret, and **Thomas2 Kidd** over a period of two months. Margaret died first in March 1727, then William2 in April 1727 and Thomas2 in May 1727. Alice, the wife of Thomas2, had died in 1720. By the summer of 1727, all of **Thomas1 Kidd's** grandchildren were orphans.

The deaths of William2 and Thomas2 in 1727 were to have a major impact on their descendants, setting into motion the transfer of all the Kidd family lands by inheritance to **Thomas3 Kidd**, the eldest son of **Thomas2 Kidd**. With no land to call their own, most of the descendants of **Margaret and William2 Kidd** left Middlesex County and headed westward across Virginia. The descendants of **Alice and Thomas2 Kidd** mainly stayed in Middlesex County or settled in nearby Essex, Caroline, and King & Queen Counties.

Based on our research of the Kidds' migration out of Middlesex County, the major Kidd families found in King & Queen County are likely to be descendants of **Thomas2 Kidd**, with origins in Middlesex, Essex, or Caroline Counties. The only known descendant of **Willliam2 Kidd** with K&Q records is **Moses Kidd**, who appears in four records between 1747 and 1751.

FREE NEGROES IN EARLY KING & QUEEN COUNTY

In the course of our research, we learned of records naming free Negroes with the surname of Kidd, beginning as early as 1813, nearly half a century before the start of the Civil War. Virtually all of these records refer to these individuals as "free Negroes" or "free Negroes and Mulattos." In this work, we use the identifier of "free Negroes" for this group of Black Virginians and their descendants.

As genealogists, we are aware of the many difficulties that Black Americans face in researching their ancestors prior to the Civil War. In this period of more than 240 years, enslaved persons had neither freedom nor legal standing. They were not enumerated or listed by name on the federal censuses; their *numbers* (along with their gender and age) were recorded, along with the number of horses, cattle and acres of property, as a measure of the wealth of the individual that owned them. Bought and sold as property, they were named in very few records.

---

[2] Dragon Swamp, also known as Dragon Run, is a major watershed that forms the headwaters of the Piankatank River. Fed by underground springs, surface runoff and numerous feeder swamps, it courses forty miles through the counties of Essex, K&Q, Middlesex and Gloucester. Its main channel serves as the boundary between Essex and Middlesex to the north, and K&Q and Gloucester to the south. See http://www.virginiaplaces.org/watersheds/dragonrun.html for more information.

Free Negros were living in K&Q County during the 18th century; the 1790 federal census for K&Q County enumerated 4,159 Whites, 75 "Free Colored," and 5,143 slaves.[3] They were artisans and famers, had the right to own property, and those who were heads of household appear in census and personal property tax records. It also should be noted that this identifier was also used for native Americans, including the Mattaponi living in local communities.[4]

In all, we found one or more records in K&Q County for 29 free Negroes with the surname of Kidd between 1747 and 1855. In the same period, we discovered one or more records for 44 white individuals. While the quantity of records created for whites far outnumber those for free Negroes, the number of these individuals with the surname of Kidd is significant in K&Q prior to the Civil War. Nor is this limited to the Kidd family: an 1833 list of free Negros in K&Q County contains the names of more than 300 individuals.[5]

---

[3] *A True Relation of the History of King and Queen County in Virginia, 1607-1790,* by Edwin **Cox**, 21 pp., 1976, p. 21.

[4] According to an archivist at the Library of Virginia, part of the reason for the large numbers of free blacks in King and Queen County were the interactions and racial confusions with the Mataponi tribe (occurring since the settlement of the area). The tribal members living on the reservation would not be listed because they were not taxed. Their relatives living off the reservation were taxed and most often listed as "mulatto," but also as "F.N." They are almost never classified as "Indian."

[5] See Appendix Two and Appendix Three of this document for more information.

SOME TIPS ON USING THIS COMPILATION

Sources used in the creation of this compilation are listed in the APPENDIX.

All URLs in this book were active as of October 10, 2020.

ABBREVIATIONS – Several abbreviations are used in this book:
K&Q – King & Queen County
LTL(s) – Land Tax List(s)   LoV – Library of Virginia
MSX – Middlesex County
PPTL(s) – Personal Property Tax List(s)

*Individuals whose names appear in **bold underlined font** have been added to the Family Tree that we are constructing on Ancestry.com, that includes all the DOCUMENTED descendants of Thomas1 Kidd of Middlesex County, Virginia. This tree can be found at:* https://www.ancestry.com/family-tree/tree/37652986/family *Once there, be sure to look in the Media Gallery of these individuals, to see what documents and other sources have been added.*

EXPLANATION OF THE GENERATIONAL NUMBERING SYSTEM WE USE

Before you get started, an explanation of the numbering system we have used in this compilation is in order: The number following an individual's name in this compilation indicates the number of generations relative to our common ancestor, Thomas1Kidd. Thus, for example, "George4 (Benjamin3, William2, Thomas1)" is short-hand for "George Kidd, 4 generations down from Thomas the immigrant, and the son of Benjamin3, grandson of William2, etc."
Again, the numbers used in this system refer to the generation of each named individual, *relative to Thomas1 Kidd*, the patriarch of our Kidd family.

Our Kidd ancestors favored several names, and repeated them in each generation; William, John, and James were used in nearly every generation, in multiple branches of a family. In order to separate these individuals with shared names but in the same location and generation, we have arbitrarily listed them as James5a, James5b, etc.

AND NOW, TO THE KIDDS OF KING & QUEEN COUNTY!

AN ALPHABETICAL LISTING OF ALL
KING & QUEEN COUNTY KIDDS BY GIVEN NAME,
THEN BY CHRONOLOGICAL APPEARANCE

The information here is freely shared with Kidd family researchers for their personal use. We ask that you credit this work or the KiddRoots.org website when using this information, and that you use it in its original form. Thank you.

ADELAIDE KIDD (1847-Dec 1849)

1850 – the 1850 mortality schedule on the K&Q federal census for St. Stephen's Parish, lists Adelaide Kidd, aged 2, death date Dec 1849. Her parents are not named in this record, and nothing more is known about her.

ANN KIDDs (see also under Nancy)

FOUR women named Ann Kidd are named in K&Q records. For the first three of these women, all their records listed their given name only as Ann. The fourth was listed as Ann in only a few records; in the others, she was named Nancy Kidd. Ann and Nancy are often used interchangeably, so it is worthwhile to review records for both given names.

1. **Ann Kidd (1) – found only on K&Q PPTLs, 1785-1794; identity unknown;**
2. **Ann Kidd (2) – the wife of John(3) Kidd;**
3. **Ann Kidd (3) – the daughter of John(3) Kidd and his wife Ann; and**
4. **Nancy/Ann Kidd – the daughter of Benjamin(3) and Nancy(1) Kidd, and sister of Benjamin F., Richard, William (W.S.), and likely Patsey (who married Thomas Hart)**

ANN KIDD (1) (in K&Q between 1785-1794)

1785-1794 – an **Ann Kidd** first appears on the K&Q PPTLs in 1785. She has no white males over 21 in the household. She's not listed in 1786 but is listed annually thereafter from 1787 through 1794. Following this, no Ann Kidd appears on these tax lists until 1831. See Tables below (two Tables are required, due to a change in column headings in 1788):

YEAR	TAXPAYER	WT	B>16	B<16	H	Cattle	COMMENTS
1785	Ann	0	8	2	2	12	8 slaves >16 (George, Will, Joe, Peter, Hanah (sic), Richmond, Charles, Gilly, tithes), 2 <16 (Daphney & Carter)
1787	Ann	0	6	3	2	10	slaves not named in 1787

It is important to note that the 1785 PPTL is our only indication of where in King County this Ann Kidd lived. Between 1783 and 1786, six tax lists were made and reported, for districts called "Hundreds." Ann Kidd appears on the list of the Third Hundred, which appears to be in the lower portion of St. Stephens Parish.[6] By comparison, John and Bartholomew Kidd were consistently found on the list of the 5th or 6th Hundred, and Henry Kidd and William Kidd were on the list of the 2nd Hundred.

YEAR	TAXPAYER	WT	B>16	B 12 -16	H	COMMENTS
1788	Ann	0	6	0	3	No slaves 12-16
1789	Ann	0	7	0	4	Wm Courtney's list
1790	Ann	0	6	0	3	Wm Courtney's list
1791	Ann	0	7	1	1	Wm Courtney's list
1792	Ann	0	8	1	1	Wm Courtney's list
1793	Ann	0	8	1	2	Wm Courtney's list
1794	Ann	0	7	1	2	Wm Courtney's list

ANN KIDD (2), the wife of John Kidd Sr. (3) [also known as John Kidd of Lumpkin and Co] of K&Q, and mother of Ann, Elizabeth, Mary Ann, Maria, Thomas, and John Kidd Jr. [John4].
Born about 1767; possible maiden name of Lumpkin (see below)
Died in 1847

Note: The K&Q LTLs for 1814 & 1815 each have two entries for John Kidd Sr. (3), where he is taxed on 178 acres owned "in fee" and bearing the notation, "Mattapony & Eubanks orphans," and taxed also on 105 acres, "part in fee and part in dower" and bearing the notations, "of Lumpkin's Estate" and "Betsy Lumpkin, adj. above land". In 1816, the acreage drops slightly by 6 acres, with no notation as to what become of the 6 acres. In 1818, the two parcels are combined and the notation "part for life" appears on the LTLs. This is evidence that the part of the Lumpkin land noted as in dower was inherited through John's wife, which means that Ann may have been a Lumpkin before her marriage.

1847 – **Ann Kidd** died 14 April 1847 in K&Q Co at the age of 80. This date comes from two sources: the Bagby family Bible[7] and a religious periodical magazine called the *Religious*

---

[6] From discussions with archivists at the Library of Virginia, it seems that in the first years of the taxes, the tax collector did not visit people's houses to collect information about taxes due, but instead set up somewhere and people came to him. In King and Queen they probably had six different regions where they held these gatherings, thus the use of the old term "hundreds." These were not so much geographical boundaries but designations of population centers. They appear to be numbered going North to South, so the 6th would be the furthest south population center. In 1786, once they went to the tax system of visiting people, they begin using parish names or district names. It appears that the 4th, 5th and 6th hundreds correspond to what is called the Lower District, B district, or Stratton Major Parish.

[7] Bagby Family Bible (1750-1860), Virginia Historical Society Acc. Mss6:4 B1465:1. A transcription of this bible is found in *Bible Records of Caroline County, Virginia Families*, by Herbert Ridgeway Collins, Heritage Books, Westminster, MD, 2008, pp. 10-ff. A card index for this (and many other Virginia family Bibles) is available at www.familysearch.org/search/collection/1932510. Once at this web page, search on either "Kidd" or "Bagby." The actual record is at the Virginia Historical Society, Cf. Mss6:4B1465:1.

Herald.

The Bagby family Bible contains these statements:

"John Kidd father of Mary Ann Bagby wife of Travis Bagby died 23 May 1839 aged 70"

"**Ann Kidd**, wife of John Kidd, and mother of Mary Ann Bagby died April 14th, 1847 aged 80 years."

The *Religious Herald* entries:

"Issue of 28 June 1839. Died, at his residence in King and Queen County, on the 23rd day of May Mr. John Kidd in the 70th year of his age."

"Issue of 22 July 1847. The **widow of brother John Kidd**...died April 14 of the current year at the residence of her son-in-law Travis Bagby, aged 80 years."

ANN KIDD (3), the daughter of John Kidd Sr. [John3 of Lumpkin and Co] and his wife, Ann(2) Kidd
    Born bet. 1786-1794[8] in K&Q. Apparently never married.
    Died testate in 1838 in K&Q

1820 – on the federal census in K&Q Co, in Stratton Major Parish:
    Ann Kidd – 2M<10, 1 10-15, 1 16-17, 1 16-25; 2F<10, 1 16-25 & 1 26-44; no slaves.

1830 – on the federal census in K&Q Co, p. 288, line 11:
    Ann Kidd – 1M 10-14 & 1 15-19; 1F 20-29 & 1 40-49; no slaves.
    Next door is Henry Kidd (see below).

    The oldest female in these two households is not old enough to be Ann(2), so more likely is Ann(3).

1831, 1837 – in these two years, an **Ann Kidd** appears on the K&Q PPTLs. At this time, the PPTLs listed only the slaves and horses a person owned, so no information about white males in the HH is available from these two entries:

YEAR	DATE	TAXPAYER	B>12	H	OTHER	COMMENTS
1831	12-Mar	Anne	0	1	1 gig ($30)	
1837	X	Anne ("N_k")	1	0		date illegible

She doesn't appear on these PPTLs after 1837.

1838 – **Ann Kidd** of K&Q signed her will on 20 May 1838. In it, she named the children of her two sisters, Elizabeth and Mary Ann, and any unborn children, as her heirs.[9]
    At the time the will was written, Elizabeth's name was Elizabeth Bagby, and she had four daughters Ann Elizabeth Motley, Mary Frances Motley and Andrewetta Motley, and Virginia Bagby. Mary Ann Bagby's[10] children were John Richard Bagby, Ann Elizabeth Bagby, and

---

[8] Judging from her entries on the 1820 and 1830 federal censuses.

[9] Lost Records Localities Digital Collection, King and Queen County, Kidd, Ann will, 1838. Library of Virginia, Richmond, VA 23219. This will can be seen online at http://www.virginiamemory.com/collections/lost and then searching on "Kidd."

[10] Mary A. Bagby died 17 Oct 1874 in Caroline Co., VA at the age of 64, according to Virginia Deaths and Burials, 1853-1917 at Ancestry.com. Her death record lists her spouse as Travis Bagby, and names her parents as "John and Ann Kidd" (citing FHL #2056976).

an unborn child at the writing of **Ann Kidd's** will, but who was subsequently named Travis Bagby (apparently after his father and Mary Ann's husband, since Mr. Travis Bagby, "my brother-in-law," was named **Ann Kidd's** executor).
Her will also bequeaths $300 to "Mr. Kidd" for caring for her while she was sick, but doesn't record his given name. Her will was admitted into court in October 1838.[11]

1839 – On 8 Nov 1839, a suit in Chancery court was heard in K&Q Co for the division of the estate of **Ann Kidd**. The purpose of the suit was to divide the estate between the children of Ann's sisters Elizabeth and Mary Ann, to establish the inheritance of Travis, the youngest child of Mary Ann Kidd Bagby (she was pregnant at the time of her sister Ann's death), and to make a division of Ann Kidd's slaves.

In a Court held for K&Q Co on Friday 8 Nov 1839:
Ann Elizabeth Motley, Mary Frances Motley, Andrewetta Motley and Virginia Bagby, children of Elizabeth Bagby; John Richard Bagby, Ann Elizabeth Bagby and Travis Bagby, children of Mary Ann Bagby, all of whom are infants under the age of twenty one years, by John Bagby their next friend, Pltfs.
against
Travis Bagby Executor of **Ann Kidd, deceased**, Deft. } In Chancery:

This cause came on this day by consent of parties to be heard upon the bill and answer, and the will of **Ann Kidd** filed as [one?] exhibit in the cause and was argued by counsel, upon consideration whereof the Court being of the opinion that the devises or bequests contained in the said will to the future children of Testatrix' two sisters, Elizabeth Bagby and Mary Ann Bagby who was *in ventre sa mere*[12] at the death of the said Testatrix
and that the estate devised or bequeathed by the said Testatrix to the children which her said sisters then had and might thereafter have vested in the children which the Testatrix's said sisters had living at the time of her death and in the said infant *in ventre sa mere*, doth therefore adjudge order and decree that the estate of **Ann Kidd deceased** be divided first into moieties [shares], and that one moiety be divided into four equal parts and the Court doth decree one of said four parts to each of the plaintiffs Elizabeth Motley, Mary Francis Motley, Andrewetta Motley and Virginia Bagby and that James M. Jeffries, John Bagby and Richard Bagby as commissioners for the purpose hereby appointed do fairly value the slaves of the estate of said **Ann Kidd** and make division of them as herein before ordered
and that in said case the said commissioners shall find that the required divisions cannot be made of the slaves in kind, that after advertising the time and place for thirty days at several of the most public places in the neighborhood, they sell one or more of the slaves as the may find necessary upon a credit of six months except as to the expenses of the sale, which they may require in cash, and that they take bonds with good security payable to such of the said parties and for such sums as will affect the required divisions and that the slaves and bonds be delivered to the guardians of those respectively entitled to them and that they report to Court their proceedings herein, and that the Defendant pay over to the guardians of the said Elizabeth Bagby's children their respective proportions of the funds in his hands. As to the

---

[11] King & Queen Chancery Cause 1840-001, online at:
http://www.lva.virginia.gov/chancery/case_detail.asp?CFN=097-1840-001 . An abstract of this estate record is available from RK (now stored in the K&Q shared folder). This will and chancery suit also cited in *Index to Virginia Estates, 1800-1865*, vol. 10, compiled by Wesley E. Pippenger, published by Virginia Genealogical Society, 2010.
[12] A French law term meaning "in the womb of its mother." Mary Ann was pregnant when her sister Ann died.

other moiety of the estate, the use thereof being bequeathed by the Testatrix to the Defendant for the term of five years, the Court doth not make any order in relation thereto at this time, and this cause is retained for future proceedings. The Court doth further order that the effect of this decree be so far suspended, that the parties or their guardians shall not be entitled to receive their portions of the estate until the Defendant shall be properly indemnified by refunding bonds if he require it. The Court doth further adjudge, order and decree that the Defendant as Exer. of said **Ann Kidd** do pay the costs of this suit.[13] [14]

1841 – In a Court held for K&Q Co on 5 May 1841.
Ann Elizabeth Motley, Mary Francis Motley, Andrewetta Motley and Virginia Bagby children of Elizabeth Bagby; John Richard Bagby, Ann Elizabeth Bagby and Travis Bagby, children of Mary Ann Bagby, all of whom are infants under the age of twenty one years by John Bagby their next friend, Plts.
against
Travis Bagby, executor of **Ann Kidd, dec'd**., Deft }In Chancery
This cause came on this day to be again heard on the papers formerly Read and the report of Commissioners having been returned more than one month and no exception having been taken thereto, it is ordered that the same be confirmed.[15]

NANCY/ANN KIDD, the daughter of Ben Kidd (3) and his wife Ann Kidd – See Nancy Kidd

BARTHOLOMEW KIDD

Born bef. 1761,[16] place and parents unknown at this time
Died ~1818 in K&Q County, Virginia

Bartholomew Kidd died without heirs, and the children of his deceased sister Anna Kidd Wilson of Fluvanna Co VA sent one of their siblings back to K&Q Co in 1823 with their power of attorney to claim their mother's inheritance. His land was located 18 miles SE of the K&Q courthouse. [Note that John(1) Kidd was enumerated in the same tax district (the 6th Hundred) as Bartholomew between 1782 and 1786, and that John(5) Kidd's land was ALSO located 18 miles SE of the K&Q Courthouse. This raises the possibility of a relationship between them.]

1782 – **Bartholomew Kidd** was taxed for 100 acres in K&Q County, the first year in which Virginia recorded land tax lists (LTLs).

1782-1818 – **Bartholomew Kidd** is found on the 1782 **PPTL** and appeared annually on these PPTLs through 1818. In the years 1795-1798, and again in 1806-1814, and 1816-1818, he

---

[13] King & Queen Chancery Cause 1840-001, online at:
http://www.lva.virginia.gov/chancery/case_detail.asp?CFN=097-1840-001 . An abstract of this estate record is available from RK (now stored in the K&Q shared folder). This will and chancery suit also cited in *Index to Virginia Estates, 1800-1865*, vol. 10, compiled by Wesley E. Pippenger, published by Virginia Genealogical Society, 2010.

[14] King & Queen Co. Order Book, 1831-1851, pp. 89-90, (LoV reel #8), reviewed by RK July 24, 2018, images 108-109. Scanned images available from the authors.

[15] King & Queen Co. Order Book, 1831-1851, p. 107 (LoV reel #8), reviewed by RK July 24, 2018, image 126. Scanned image available upon request.

[16] Judging from his appearance on the 1782 K&Q PPTL, when he had to be at least 21 years old to be listed.

pays annual tithes on 2 white males; all other years he's taxed just for himself. The second white tithe in these years is not known. See Tables[17] below:

YEAR	TAXPAYER	WT	B>16	B<16	H	Cattle	COMMENTS
1782	Bartholomew	1	2	1	2	7	slaves not named
1783	Bartholomew	1	2	4	3	7	6 slaves named (Eliza., Wm., Cato, Phillis, Sally, Fanny), but 7 total souls; One WT, but NO white souls.
1784	Bartholomew	1	2	2	3	7	4 named slaves: Cato & Fillis, Tythes;Sary & Fanny (<16)
1785	Bartholomew	1	3	1	2	9	Slaves Cate, Fillis, Sal, Fan
1786	Bartholomew	1	3	1	1	8	Slaves Catto, Phillis, Sall, Fanny
1787	Bartholomew	1	3	1	2	10	slaves not named in 1787

YEAR	TAXPAYER	WT	B>16	B 12 -16	H	Cows	COMMENTS
1788	Bartholomew	1	3	0	2	-	No slaves 12-16
1789	Bartholomew	1	3	0	2	-	Wm Fleet's list
1790	Bartholomew	1	2	0	2	-	Wm Fleet's list
1791	Bartholomew	1	3	0	2		Wm Fleet's list
1792	Bartholomew	1	2	0	2		Wm Fleet's list
1793	Bartholomew	1	2	0	2		Wm Fleet's list
1794	Bartholomew	2	2	0	2		Wm Fleet's list
1795	Bartholomew	2	2	0	2		Wm Fleet's list
1796	Bartholomew	2	2	1	2		Beverly Roy's list
1797	Bartholomew	2	2	1	2		Beverly Roy's list
1798	Bartholomew	2	2	1	2		Beverly Roy's list
1799	Bartholomew	1	2	1	2		Beverly Roy's list
1800	Bartholomew	1	2	1	3		Beverly Roy's list
1801	Bartholomew	1	1	1	3		Wm Fleet's list
1802	Bartholomew	1	2	1	3		Shackelford's list

---

[17] Two tables are required because the format for listing the information for each individual changed over time.

1803	Bartholomew	1	2	1	3		Shackelford's list
1804	Bartholomew	1	2	1	3		Shackelford's list
1805	Bartholomew	1	2	1	2		Spencer's list
1806	Bartholomew	2	3	1	2		Spencer's list
1807	Bartholomew	2	3	1	2		Spencer's list
1809	Bartholomew	2	4	1	2		Faulkner's list
1810	Bartholomew	2	4	1	2		Faulkner's list
1811	Bartholomew	2	4	1	2		Faulkner's list
1812	Bartholomew	2	5	0	3		Faulkner's list
1813	Bartholomew	2	5	0	3		Faulkner's list
1814	Bartholomew	2	5	0	3		Fleet's list
1815	Bartholomew	1	4	0	3	58	Francis Row's L
1816	Bartholomew	2	4	0	3		Francis Row's L
1817	Bartholomew	2	4	0	3		Francis Row's L
1818	Bartholomew	2	4	0	3		Francis Row's L
1819	Bartholomew Est	0	4	1	1		Francis Row's L
1820	Bartholomew Est	0	4	1	1		Francis Row's L

1787-1818 – the K&Q **LTL** of 1787 shows that **Bartholomew Kidd** is taxed for 136 acres in K&Q. This continues through 1818. See the Table below for his LTL listings.

Year	NAME	Acres	Description	CH	COMMENTS
1782	Bartholomew Kidd	100	(none)		
1783-1786	Not Listed		"near Guthrie & Halbert"		Sold land to Edward Brook in 1785, judging from Alterations that year.
1787-1797	Bartholomew Kidd	136			"from Edwin Walden," per *Colonial VA Abstracts*, v4, p. 43
1798-1802	Bartholomew Kidd	136 132½			- "from Wm Dillard Jr."
1803-1810	Bartholomew Kidd	136 132½ 95½			- "from Wm Dillard Jr." "from Robert Lumpkin"
1811-1812	Bartholomew Kidd	136 228			- from Wm Dillard & R.Lumpkin
1813	Bartholomew Kidd	136 228			- from Wm Dillard & R.Lumpkin

Year	NAME	Acres	Description	CH	COMMENTS
1814-1816	Bartholomew Kidd	136 228	Jno. Bland the younger	18SE	- from Wm Dillard & R.Lumpkin
1817	Bartholomew Kidd	136 228 48	Jno. Bland the younger	18SE	- - by deed from Tabitha & Sally Walden
1818	Bartholomew Kidd	136 228 48 48	All adj to Jno Bland the younger	18SE	- - - by deed from S& wife, and Eliza Walden
1819-1820	Bartholomew Kidd's Estate	136 228 48 48	All adj to Jno Bland the younger	18SE	
1821-1823	Bartholomew Kidd's Estate	460	Jno Bland (Y)	18SE	(all 4 tracts combined)
1824	Drops from LTLs				The children of his deceased sister Anna Kidd Wilson claimed their inheritance in 1823.

[Note: Just before his death, Bartholomew purchased two tracts of 48 acres each, from people with connections to the Walden family.]

1810 – on federal census in K&Q Co., p. 222B, line 8

Bartholomew Kidd – 1M 16-25 & 1 45 and up; 1F 16-25 & 1 45 and up, plus 6 slaves. [We do not know the identity of the members of Bartholomew's HH.]

1819-1823 – In 1819, **Bartholomew Kidd** 's entry on the annual K&Q PPTLs is for his estate. This entry continues through 1823. Then in 1824, there is no entry for Bartholomew's estate. This coincides with the 1823 Fluvanna Co VA Power of Attorney filed by the nieces and nephews of Bartholomew Kidd (see next entry).

1823 – In a power of attorney dated 25 Oct 1823 and recorded 27 Oct 1823 in Fluvanna Co VA, Walker Wilson and the other heirs of Anna Kidd Wilson give power of attorney to their brother Barnett Wilson to receive their interest "in an estate left my deceased mother, left her by her brother **Bartholomew Kidd**, deceased of the County of King and Queen." The heirs are named in the POA as "David Ross (who intermarried with Frances Wilson), William Sadler (who intermarried with Rachel Wilson), John White (who intermarried with Sarah Wilson), David White who intermarried with Rebecca Wilson), Barnett Wilson, John Wilson, Walker Wilson, and Elizabeth Wilson by her guardian Barnett Wilson all of the County of Fluvanna and the State of Virginia, children and heirs of Anna Wilson decd, formerly Anna Kidd".[18]

BENJAMIN KIDD(s)

There were three men named Benjamin Kidd in K&Q between 1787 and 1815; we have distinguished between them by where in the county they lived and whether they owned land.

Benjamin Kidd (1) – "of MSX"; married Mary Guthrie; owned slaves but not land in K&Q; records in K&Q between 1787 and 1789.

Benjamin Kidd (2) – also identified as "of MSX" in some records; owned slaves and land in the SE part of K&Q; left records in K&Q between 1787 and 1809. This man is Benjamin Kidd, son of James and Mary Kidd of Middlesex Co VA.

Benjamin Kidd (3) - Lived 9 miles NE of the Courthouse; wife was Nancy/Ann(3); left records in K&Q between 1796 and 1815.

BENJAMIN KIDD (1), listed as "of Middlesex" when he married Mary Guthrie in 1784 in K&Q County

1784-1785 – a **Benjamin Kidd** first appears on the annual PPTLs of K&Q Co. in 1784, then again in 1785.

YEAR	TAXPAYER	WT	B>16	B<16	H	Cattle	COMMENTS
1784	Benjamin		0	1	2	6	slave, Jupiter <16
1785	Benjamin	1	0	0	1	3	

He's not on these PPTLs in 1786. See 1787, below.

1784 – a **Benjamin Kidd** married Mary Guthrie, apparently in K&Q Co, according to *Some Marriages in the Burned Record Counties of Virginia*, by the Virginia Genealogical Society.[19] The date of this marriage was 8 January 1784.[20] The marriage was recorded in Middlesex Co Christ Church Parish, noting **Benjamin Kidd** was of Middlesex Co, and Mary Guthrie was of K&Q Co. [See next entry.]

1784 – Mary Guthrie married **Benjamin Kidd** on January 8 of this year. At the end of page 205 of the CCP Register is written: "The above drawn off for the Clerks of those County's wherein the above Marriages were solemnized." Kidd marriages listed on page 205 are **Benjamin Kidd** to Mary Guthrie dated 1784, and three dated 1786: William Kidd to Rachel Chowning, Lucy Kidd (King and Queen) to Thomas Lambeth, and Henry Kidd to Catherine Swords [Seward]. Only the notations for Mary Guthrie and Lucy Kidd say King and Queen specifically, but we can infer that these four marriages took place in K&Q Co.[21]

---

[18] Fluvanna Co VA Deed Book 8, p. 372. Titled "Power of Attorney, Wilson to Wilson."

[19] Page 23, citing the Christ Church Parish Register, p. 263.

[20] *Some Marriages in the Burned Record Counties of Virginia*, VA Genealogical Society Special Publication #4.

[21] *Parish Register of Christ Church Parish, Middlesex Co., Virginia, 1635-1812*, p 205.

1787-1789 – A **Benjamin Kidd Jr.** appears on the K&Q PPTLs for these three years. In 1787, there are two Benjamins: one noted as Benjamin Jr., believed to be Benjamin (1), and the second noted as Benjamin, believed to be Benjamin (2). See Table below:

YEAR	TAXPAYER	WT	B>16	B<16	H	Cattle	COMMENTS
1787	Benjamin	1	2	2	2	0	slaves not named in 1787; one WM 16-21
1787	Benjamin Jr.	1	0	1	1	7	slaves not named in 1787
YEAR	TAXPAYER	WT	B>16	B 12 -16	H	Cows	COMMENTS
1788	Benjamin Jr.	1	0	0	1	-	catttle dropped
1788	Benjamin MDX	1	1	0	0	-	Ben of MDX chargable with the tax; John Kidd was the 1 WMT
1789	Benjamin	1	0	0	2	-	Wm Fleet's list
1789	Benjamin MDX	0	1	1	1	-	Wm Fleet's list; no WMT in HH this yr

BENJAMIN KIDD (2), of MSX Co, son of James and Mary Kidd of Urbanna in MSX Co. Owned land in SE K&Q Co but was a resident of MSX Co.

1787 – Land Alterations records from the 1787 K&Q Co Land Tax List show that **Benjamin Kidd** received from Richard "Walding" [Walden] a tract of 75 acres in K&Q Co.[22]

1787-1789 – A **Benjamin Kidd** appears for the first time in 1787 on the K&Q **LTLs**, taxed upon 111 acres. In 1788-1789, his entry is followed by the notation "(Middlesex)," evidently indicating that he resided in MSX Co.

1787 – A second **Benjamin Kidd** appears on the K&Q PPTLs in 1787. This is likely Benjamin (2); the first, noted as Benjamin Jr., is believed to be Benjamin (1).
SEE THE TABLE, ABOVE.

1788-1789 – In 1788, the K&Q **PPTL** shows that **Benjamin Kidd** of "MDX" (Middlesex County) paid the tithe for a John Kidd, but not one for himself, indicating he was not a K&Q Co resident. John Kidd may have been the caretaker or overseer of Benjamin's land in K&Q Co, possibly related to this Benjamin Kidd. In 1789, John is not listed, and Benjamin (MSX) pays no white tithes, again indicating he was not a K&Q resident.

1791-1792 – in each of these years, the same **Benjamin Kidd** appears annually on the K&Q **LTLs**, and the entries continue to list him as "Middlesex." But in each of these years, he's now charged tax on three separate parcels of land: 1) a 41-acre parcel (apparently the residue of the 111-acre parcel that he was taxed on 1787-1795); 2) a 60-acre parcel bearing the notation,

---

[22] *Virginia Colonial abstracts*, volume 4, by Beverley Fleet, p. 43.

"of Crittenden" (this appears to be land previously belonging to Thomas Crittenden, who married Jane Kidd, the daughter of James Kidd Sr.; this Jane was Benjamin Kidd's sister); and 3) a 36-acre parcel bearing the notation "Dragon Swamp." This land lay on the boundary between King and Queen County and Middlesex Co.

1793-1795 – His annual K&Q LTLs change again, returning to the listings of 1787-1790 (the only difference being that he's again taxed on 111 acres in parcel #1; the others are unchanged).

1796-1804 – in 1796, the K&Q LTL entries for **Benjamin Kidd** drop the "Middlesex" notation, but the land parcels are unchanged from prior years. The listings continue thus through 1804.

1805-1809 – in 1805, the K&Q LTL listing for this **Benjamin Kidd** changes, no longer listing the 60-acre parcel; he continues to be taxed on the other two parcels, of 111 and 36 acres, respectively in 1805, 1806 and 1807. The 36-acre tract was on Dragon Swamp,[23] according to the notation.
In 1808, no taxes were collected in the state of Virginia.
In 1809, he was taxed on only 25 acres in K&Q. [This entry could belong to either Benjamin (2) or Benjamin(3).]

This **Benjamin Kidd** of Middlesex Co drops from the K&Q LTLs in 1810 and isn't found there in 1811 or 1812.

BENJAMIN KIDD (3), birthplace and parents unknown
Born no later than 1775
Married Nancy _____ (last name not known)
Lived in northeastern K&Q County, 9 miles NE of the Courthouse
Died by 1815, K&Q County, Virginia
Father of Benjamin F., Richard, Nancy (Ann), William S., and likely Patsey (who married Thomas Hart)[24]

1796-1814 – a **Benjamin Kidd** appears annually on the K&Q **PPTLs**, each time paying just one white male tithe. In 1815, his estate appears, indicating that he has died in the past 12 months.

YEAR	TAXPAYER	WT	B>16	B 12 -16	H	Cows	COMMENTS
1796	Benjamin	1	0	0	0		Beverly Roy's list
1797	Benjamin	1	0	0	0		Beverly Roy's list
1798	Benjamin	1	0	0	0		Beverly Roy's list
1799	Benjamin	1	0	0	0		Beverly Roy's list
1800	Benjamin	1	0	0	0		Beverly Roy's list

---

[23] Dragon Swamp, also known as Dragon Run, is a brackish water tidal/nontidal stream that forms the headwaters of the Piankatank River. Fed by underground springs, surface runoff and numerous feeder swamps, it courses forty miles through the counties of Essex, K&Q, Middlesex and Gloucester. Its main channel serves as the boundary between Essex and Middlesex to the north, and K&Q and Gloucester to the south. See http://www.virginiaplaces.org/watersheds/dragonrun.html for more information.

[24] All of whom received parts of the land he owned after his death, per the K&Q Land Tax Lists.

1801	Benjamin	1	0	0	0		Wm Fleet's list
1802	Benjamin	1	0	0	0		Shackelford's list
1803	Benjamin	1	1	0	0		Shackelford's list
1804	Benjamin	1	0	0	0		Shackelford's list
1805	Benjamin	1	0	0	0		Spencer's list
1806	Benjamin Sr.	1	0	0	1		Spencer's list
1806	Benjamin Jr.	1	0	0	0		Spencer's list
1807	Benjamin	1	0	0	0		Spencer's list
1809	Benjamin	1	1	0	0		Faulkner's list
1810	Benjamin	1	1	0	0		Faulkner's list
1811	Benjamin	1	1	0	0		Faulkner's list
1812	Benjamin	1	1	0	1		Faulkner's list
1813	Benjamin	1	0	0	0		Faulkner's List
1814	Benjamin	1	1	0	1		Fleet's list
1815	Benjamin, Est.	0	1	0	2	7	Francis Row's L

1809 – A **Benjamin Kidd** is listed in the K&Q LTL with a 25-acre tract. [This entry could belong to either Benjamin (2) or Benjamin(3).]

1810 – on federal census in K&Q Co., p. 221 (mis-indexed as RIDD)
Benjamin Kidd: 1M<10 & 1 26-44; 3F<10 & 1 26-44, with one slave.

1813-1815 – a **Benjamin Kidd** again is found on the K&Q LTLs in each of these years, now charged for 56 acres "in fee," adjacent to Jno. Oliver. In 1815, this land is recorded as 9 miles NE of K&Q Courthouse, placing it closest to Essex Co.:

Year	NAME	Acres	Description	CH	COMMENTS
1813	Benjamin Kidd	56			
1814-1815	Benjamin Kidd	56	Adj. Jno. Oliver	9NE	

1815 – In this year, **Benjamin Kidd's** entry on the K&Q PPTL is for his estate, indicating that he's died in the past twelve months. He then drops from these annual lists. See the PPTL Table above.

1816 – In this year, **Benjamin Kidd's** estate appears on the LTLs. It remains on the LTLs at least through 1863, the last year we've checked the LTLs:

Year	NAME	Acres	Description	CH	COMMENTS
1816-1840	Benjamin Kidd Est.	56	Adj. Jno. Oliver	9NE	
1841					Pages with Ks missing

Year	NAME	Acres	Description	CH	COMMENTS
1842-1849	Benjamin Kidd Est.	56	Adj. Martha Oliver	9NE	
1850					Pages with Ks missing
1851-1854	Benjamin Kidd Est.	56	Thomas Hundley	9NE	
1855-1859	Benjamin Kidd Est.	56	Edward Gresham	9NE	
1860	Benjamin Kidd Est.	48	Edward Gresham	9NE	8 acres to Ann Kidd
1861-1863	Benjamin Kidd Est.	48	E. Gresham's Est.	9NE	Aft. 1861, neighbor was Edw. Gresham's Tract

BENJAMIN F. KIDD, the son of Benjamin Kidd (3) above, and his wife Nancy.
> **Born ca 1812, most likely in K&Q County, Virginia**
> **Married Eliza ___ (last name unknown)**
> **Lived in northeastern K&Q County, 9 miles NE of the Courthouse, as did his father before him**
> **Died 11 August 1854 in Henrico Co VA, predeceasing his mother, Nancy**

1838-1852 – In 1838, a new **Benjamin Kidd** appears on the K&Q **PPTLs**, more than 20 years since a Benjamin Kidd last appeared. He appears annually (missing only in 1842) through 1852, each time paying 1 white male tithe, then disappears from these tax lists.

Year	TAXPAYER	WMT	B>12	B>16	H	COMMENTS
1838	Kidd, Benjamin	NA[25]	0	0	1	
1839	Kidd, Benjamin	NA	0	0	1	
1840	Kidd, Benjamin	NA	0	0	1	1 gig ($20)
1841	Kidd, Benjamin	1	0	0	0	
1842	Not listed					
1843	Kidd, Benjamin	1	0	0	1	
1844	Kidd, Benjamin	1	1	1	1	
1845	Kidd, Benjamin	1	0	0	1	1 gig ($40)
1846	Kidd, Benjamin	1	0	1	1	1 gig ($25), 1 clock
1847	Benjamin Kidd	1	1	1	1	1 metallic clock
1848	Benjamin Kidd	1	1	0	1	1 metallic clock

---

[25] The PPTLs for 1838-1840 did not record the number of white male tithes; this began in 1841.

1849	Benjamin Kidd	1	2	1	2	gold watch
1850	Benjamin Kidd	1	2	1	1	1 metallic clock
1851	Benj. F. Kidd	1	1	1	1	1 4-wh carriage ($50), 1 metallic clock
1852	Benjamin Kidd	1	0	0	1	29 cows, sheep, hogs; buggy ($25), metallic clock
1853	Drops from lists					

1840 – No **Benjamin Kidd** found on the federal census in K&Q Co.

1843 - **Benjamin Kidd** was charged with a tax of $ .50 in K&Q Co for serving as administrator of Henry Hillyard, dec'd.[26]

1844, ff. – **Benjamin Kidd** appears on the K&Q **LTLs** in 1844 for the first time, taxed on 26½ acres adjacent to Ann Newbill and John Motley, 9 miles NE of the courthouse.
His land was very near the Benjamin Kidd estate; John Motley's LTL entry notes Motley's land was adjacent to the land of the Benjamin Kidd estate. He appears on the LTLs until 1853.

Year	NAME	Acres	Description	CH	COMMENTS
1844-1849	Benjamin Kidd	26½	adj Ann Newbill & John Motley	9NE	
1850	-	-	-	-	Pages with Ks missing
1851	Benjamin Kidd	26½	adj Ann Newbill & John Motley	9NE	
1852-1853	Benjamin Kidd	26½	adj Ann Newbill & John Motley	9NE	
		81		9NE	"from Henry Williams' Est."
1854	Drops from LTLs				

1850 – Benjamin Kidd (mis-indexed on Ancestry.com as RIDD) appears on the federal census in St. Stephen's Parish, K&Q Co, p. 156, HH 121/121:
Kidd, Benjamin F. 37MW millwright $500 VA
Next door on one side is John M. Thruston, age 34 with wife Elizabeth and two young sons, and on the other is Holt Richerson, age 34 and his family. This correlates with the listings

---

[26] "1843 List of Deeds and Probates, King and Queen County," by Wesley E. Pippenger, FVGS, appearing in *Virginia Magazine of Genealogy*, vol. 54(1), 2016, page 23.

on the 1850 census slave schedules, where Thruston and Richerson are Kidd's immediate neighbors.

In 1850, the K&Q Co census slave schedules for **Benja F. Kidd** list one female aged 50, one male aged 40, one female aged 15, and one female aged 10.

1851 – Two Benjamin Kidds, one noted as Benjamin F. and one as Benjamin, appear on the K&Q PPTLs for one year, in 1851. The identity of the second Benjamin Kidd is unknown.

1851-1853 – A new entry for **Benjamin Kidd** appears on the K&Q LTLs, but does not appear in 1854.

Year	NAME	Acres	Description	CH	COMMENTS
1851-1853	Benjamin Kidd & Christopher Carleton	26	Adj R.H. Dickenson	9NE	

1854 – **Benjamin Kidd** does not appear on the K&Q LTL for this year. He has sold his land, as noted in the Land Tax Alterations list; during the past 12 months, he sells 68½ acres to John Motley, who then sells the land to John Thurston, 8 NE. Benjamin also sells 43½ acres to John H. Thurston, for a total of 112 acres.

1854 – **Benjamin F. Kidd** died 11 August 1854 in Henrico Co VA. [27] [28] His death record states that he died aged 42 years of consumption (pulmonary tuberculosis), that he was born in King & Queen County, and was **the son of Benj. and Nancy Kidd**. Eliza Kidd, his wife, was the informant for this record, and listed as the household head.
His occupation was listed as millwright.

BILLY KIDD(s), free Negroes

Judging from the K&Q PPTLs, there were at least two (and possibly 3) free Negroes by this name, appearing on these tax lists between 1813 and 1855: two appearing simultaneously in 1813, and the reappearance of a Billy Kidd, free Negro in 1842-1855.

1813-1818 – In 1813, free Negroes with the surname of Kidd appear for the first time on the K&Q PPTLs. In this year, eleven individuals, 10 males and one female, are found on one of the two tax lists; as the table below depicts, two of them were **Billy Kidd** and **Billy Kidd, Jr.**

YEAR	LIST	NAME	NOTATION
1813	A	Billy Kidd	"free Negro"
1813	A	Billy Kidd Jr.	"free Negro"
1814	A	Billy Kidd	"free Negro"
1815	A & B	no F. N. listed	
1816	A	Billy Kidd	"free Negro"

---

[27] Pippenger (v. 7, p. 379), citing Henrico WB 14, p. 511 (inventory) and p. 517 (sale), and WB 16:313 & 337 (final account, 1859).

[28] Henrico Co. Death Registers, 1853-1896, FHL # 2056983. Scanned image available upon request (stored in the Henrico folder on Dropbox).

1817		Not listed	
1818	B	Billy Kidd	"free Negro"

1819-1841 – In 1819, **Billy Kidd**, free Negro, drops from the PPTLs in K&Q. This name isn't found again until 1842 (see below), although other free Negroes are listed.

1833 – Neither Billy Kidd nor William Kidd appear on the 1833 list of Free Negroes living in K&Q. See Appendix Two for details about that list.

1842-1855 – In 1842, for the first time in over 20 years, the name of a **Billy Kidd** reappears on the K&Q PPTLs (see table below). This is likely a different younger man. He appears in many but not all years during this time.

YEAR	TAXPAYER	NOTATION
1842	Billy Kidd	"free Negro"
1843	Billy Kidd	"free Negro"
1847	Billy Kidd	"free Negro"
1849	Billy Kidd	"free Negro"
1850	Billy Kidd	"free Negro"
1855	Billy Kidd	"free Negro"

In 1847, 1849 and 1850, his entry seems to indicate that he owned two slaves, but no horses.

1855 – At a Circuit Court for K&Q County on 16 November 1855, on the motion of James W. Courtney who made oath, and with John M. Burton his security who justified on oath as to his sufficiency, entered into and acknowledged a bond in the penalty of one thousand dollars conditioned according to law, Certificate is granted to said James W. Courtney for obtaining letters of administration of the Estate of **Billy Kidd, deceased** in due form.
Ordered that Andrew Wyatt, James Guthrie, James H. Henry and John W. Bulman or any three of them … do appraise the estate of **Billy Kidd**, deceased and return the appraisment thereof to this court.[29]

1856 – At a Circuit Court for K&Q County on 17 November 1856, an appraisment of the estate of **Billy Kidd**, deceased, was returned to court and ordered to be recorded. Also on this date, an account of sales of his estate was returned and recorded. The entry contains no details from either record.[30]

1856 – the inventory of the estate of **William Kidd** of Point View and sale of the estate of **Billy Kidd** are recorded in K&Q Co in Circuit Superior Court papers. Because these records are on adjoining pages, it is presumed they pertain to the same individual.[31]

---

[29] King and Queen County Order Book, 1854-1867, page 32, retrieved from FHL #32118, image 56, via familysearh.org (unrestricted access). Image available upon request.

[30] King and Queen County Order Book, 1854-1867, page 58, retrieved from FHL #32118, image 82, via familysearh.org (unrestricted access). Image available upon request.

[31] *Index to Virginia Estates, 1800-1865*, vol. 10, compiled by Wesley E. Pippenger, published by Virginia Genealogical Society, 2010, citing Circuit Superior Court of Law, Accounts, Administrations, 184[1]-1897, citing p. 18 for sale of Billy Kidd estate and p. 19 for inventory of estate of William Kidd of Point View. Due to courthouse fires, this is one of the few surviving county records pre-1864.

No further mentions of him were discovered in our research. He is never found as a household head on the federal censuses.

<u>CATHERINE F. KIDD</u>, the daughter of Lee Boulware (1777-1839) and his wife, Catherine F. Miller (1786-1864)
Born in 1815 (per her headstone; see below)
Married John M. Kidd (John Kidd (4) in this compilation)
Widowed by 1837, with two small children; lived with her mother in years after
Died in 1865 in K&Q (see below)
Children were Maria Louisa Kidd and John B. Kidd

1837-1855 – A **Catherine Kidd** first appears on the King & Queen Co VA **PPTLs** in 1837, with the notation "(relict [widow] of Jno. Jr.)." [32] He died in 1836. She continues to appear on the King & Queen Co VA PPTLs through 1855, the last year that we have checked.
She has no white male tithes until 1853, when 1 WMT appears in her household for three years, 1853-1855. This is likely her son John B., born in 1836.

YEAR	DATE	TAXPAYER	B>12	H	OTHER	COMMENTS
1837	X	Catherine	0	0	relict of Jno. Jr.?[33]	date illegible
1838	X	Catherine	0	0	1 gig, $40	
1839	X	Catherine	0	0	1 gig ($30)	
1840	X	Catherine	1	0	1 gig, $25	

YEAR	DATE	TAXPAYER	WMT	B>12	B>16	H	COMMENTS
1841	5-Apr	Catherine F.	0	1	1	0	1 buggy ($100)
1842	23-Feb	Catherine F.	0	1	1	0	1 4-wh riding carriage
1843	15-Jun	Catherine F.	0	1	1	0	1 4-wh riding carriage
1844	7-Mar	Catherine F.	0	1	1	0	1 gig ($50)
1845	x	Catherine F.	0	1	1	0	1 4-wh carriage; also taxed on profits upon money loaned ($100)
1846	x	Catherine F.	0	1	1	0	1 4-wh carriage; also taxed on profits upon money loaned ($100)
1847	x	Catherine F.	0	1	1	0	1 4-wh carriage; 1 gold watch; tax upon money loaned ($100)

---

[32] An image of this entry is available upon request.
[33] Ibid.

1848	4-Feb	Catherine F.	0	1	1	0	1 2-wh carriage ($20), I gold watch
1849	x	Catherine F.	0	1	1	0	4-wh pleasure carriage; 1 gold watch; piano ($150), $220 income
1850	x	Catherine F.	0	1	1	0	as before
1851	27-Feb	Catherine F.	0	1	1	0	(as before)

1838 – **Catherine Kidd** had a school in the Newtown area:
> Mrs. William Boulware, of Traveller's Rest, in a letter to a Washington friend in 1838, wrote that the recently widowed "**Catherine Kidd** has taken the school that Caroline bought last year" and in the fall of the same year that "**Catherine Kidd** and Lee Boulware are getting on very well with their schools." [34] (Caroline is Caroline Boulware Broaddus, Catherine's sister, and Lee Boulware her brother.)

1840 – We believe that she is living with her mother, Catherine F. Boulware, in New Town, K&Q County at the time of the 1840 census:[35]
> Catherine F. Boulware: 1M<5, 1 1 20-29; & 1 30-39; 1F 5-9, one 15-19, 3F 20-29, & 1 40-49. Twenty-five slaves.
> Catherine F. Kidd, widowed 3 years earlier, would be one of the 3 females age 20-29, and the two young children here are her two children, John B. (born abt 1836) and Maria Louisa, (born abt 1834).

1850 – on the federal census in Drysdale Parish, K&Q Co, p. 200, HH 848:
> Boulware, Kiturah [Catherine, her mother] 63FW (no occupation listed) $4300 VA
> Broaddus, Caroline37FW VA
> **Kidd, Catherine F**. 36FW VA
> " , Maria Louisa 16FW VA
> " , John B. 14MW VA
> Broaddus, Wm. Lee 3MW VA
> Taliaferro, Catherine L. 8FW VA

YEAR	DATE	NAME	WM >16	B >16	WM >21	B >12	H	COMMENTS
1852	1-Jul	Catherine F.	0	1	0	1	0	buggy ($75). Gold watch ($50), piano ($125); interest
1853	1-Jun	Catherine F.	1	1	0	0	0	similar to before

---

[34] *Bulletin of the King & Queen County Historical Society of Virginia*, #13, July 1962, column 6. The K&Q Historical Society's web page is at http://www.kingandqueenmuseum.com . They are in the process of indexing all the issues of their newsletter, and are currently up to #111, as of April 2012. FYI, the number references to bulletins 1-50 are by column number, 51-100 by page number.

[35] Parnassus Bird was the enumerator of this census; he was also the tax enumerator for several of Catherine F. Kidd's entries on the K&Q PPTLs.

1854	3-May	Catherine F.	1	1	0	0	1	as before
1855	22-Feb	Catherine F.	1	1	0	0	0	as before

This is the last year of the K&Q PPTLs that we've examined to date.

1860 – on the federal census in K&Q Co VA, New Town PO, p. 11, HH 84, living alone:
Kidd, Catherine F. 48FW (no occupation listed) $6800 (personal estate) VA

Next door is Catherine F. Boulware, 75FW, Catherine's mother and also a wealthy woman ($6000/$11,056) born in VA. In Boulware's HH is William L. Broaddus, a 14WM, the same boy as seen in 1850.

1865 – **Catherine Kidd** evidently died in 1865, according to correspondence from the K&Q Historical Society, stating that she is buried in the Bates (Boulware) cemetery[36] near Newtown (along with her daughter Maria Louisa, her parents Lee and Catherine F. Boulware, and her Boulware siblings):
Maria Louisa Kidd (1834-1853)
Lee Boulware (17?? -)
Catherine F. Boulware (1786-1864)
Sons
John (1809-1831)
William (1811-1870)
Lee (1819)
Daughters
C.W. Broaddus (Caroline Boulware) (1813-1852)
C.F. Kidd (Catherine Boulware) (1815-1865)
A.N. Lumpkin (Amanda Boulware) (1817-1880)
S.M. Taliaferro (Susan Boulware) (1821-1896)
This society has **Catherine Kidd's** account book for 1864-1865 in their archives.

DICK KIDD, free Negro

1813-1816 – As demonstrated by the table below, a free Negro by the name of Dick Kidd appears on the PPTLs of K&Q in each of these years except 1815, when no free Negroes are listed:

Year	TAXPAYER	NOTATION
1813	Dick Kidd	"free Negro"
1814	Dick Kidd	"free Negro"
1816	Dick Kidd	"free Negro"

He drops from these lists in 1817, and isn't found again through 1855, the last year of these records that we have reviewed.
We have not found any other references to him in K&Q records.

---

[36] *The King & Queen County Historical Society Bulletin*, #25 (July 1968), page 6, in an article about tombstones in K&Q County.

EDMUND KIDD – only one record found to date for Edmund Kidd in K&Q Co:

1787 – **Edmund Kidd** appears on the membership list (p. 8 of the minute book) for Upper King and Queen Baptist Church on July 6, listed as "Dismist." Directly above Edmund Kidd's name appears that of John Kidd, listed as "Dismist" followed by "Returned."[37] Other Kidd individuals mentioned in these church records are Fanny Kidd, Molley Kidd, William Kidd, Sr. and William Kidd Jr.[38]

EDWARD/NED KIDD, free Negro in K&Q, 1813-1820

1814-1820 – A free Negro by the name of Edward Kidd appears on the K&Q PPTLs from 1814-1820.

YEAR	TAXPAYER	NOTATION
1813	Ned Kidd	
1814	Edward Kidd	"free Negro"
1815	No FN listed this yr.	
1816	Ned Kidd	
1817	Only 1 FN this yr.	
1818	Edward Kidd	"free Negro"
1819	No FN listed this yr.	
1820	Edward Kidd	"free Negro"

In each of these years, Edward/Ned were charged only for his own tax. Neither of them were listed as owning a horse in these years.

Since Edward and Ned never appear simultaneously in any given year, and since Ned is a common nickname for Edward, we believe that Edward and Ned Kidd were one and the same.

Neither name is found again on the K&Q PPTLs after 1820, and no other records have been found for either Edward or Ned Kidd, a free Negro.

ELIZA KIDD, a free Black woman in 1850

1850 – Eliza Kidd, a free Black woman, appears on the federal census in K&Q Co, Stratton Major Parish, in the household of Polly Kidd, a free black woman and perhaps her mother. They are living among both black and white neighbors.

p 180B, dwelling 531, HH 531:
Kidd, Polly [mis-indexed as Kadd] 50 FB no occupation listed VA
  " , Milly Ann 5 FB VA
  " , John 4 MB VA
  " , **Eliza** 24 FB VA
  " , George 3 MB VA

---

[37] *Upper King and Queen Baptist Church Records, King and Queen County, 1774-1788*, transcribed by Richard Slatten and Edgar MacDonald, published in Virginia Genealogical Society *Quarterly*, vol. 30, no. 1, p. 63, February 1992.
[38] *Magazine of Virginia Genealogy*, volume 30, pp. 63-64.

We have found no other mentions of her in K&Q records.

ELIZABETH KIDD, (b bef 1775), lived in St. Stephens Parish in the NW part of K&Q.

1820 – **Elizabeth Kidd** is a head of household on the federal census in K&Q Co, St. Stephens Parish, p 15: 1 WM 16-25, 1 WF 16-25, and 1 WF 45+. There were 7 slaves were 1 M under 14, 1 M 14-25, 2 M 26-44, 1 M 45+, 1 F under 14, 1 F 45+. There were 4 persons engaged in agriculture.

There is no Elizabeth Kidd listed on the K&Q Co PPTLs in this timeframe. The white male in her household of taxable age may be listed on the PPTLs, although his name is unknown.

<u>ELIZABETH KIDD MOTLEY</u> (ca 1770 – after 1830), the daughter of William Kidd Sr. of Caroline County, Virginia
Born abt. 1770, most likely in Caroline County
Married Edwin Motley in Caroline County in 1794; widowed by 1810
Died after 1830, probably in K&Q County

1794 – **Elizabeth Kidd** married Edwin Motley in Caroline Co VA on 13 Dec 1794.[39], [40]

1802 – Caroline County Chancery Court records show that William Kidd Sr. of Caroline Co died testate in 1802, leaving a widow, Mary Kidd, and eleven children: James, **Elizabeth (who married Edwin Motley)**, Fanny (who married Washington Jones), John, Edmund, Joel, William, Philip, Walker, and Polly, plus one grandson, Henry Kidd, the only child of William Kidd, deceased. Walker, Henry and Polly are infants at the time of this record, and Thomas and Philip are administrators of William's will. Chancery Court records show that Elizabeth's younger brother, James Kidd, died before their father died in 1802, and one of James's orphan sons, William Kidd, was taken in and raised by **Edwin and Elizabeth Motley**.[41]

1804-1810 – In 1804, the estate of Elizabeth's father was distributed among his heirs, and she (via her husband) received her 26-acre share, per the Caroline Co Land Tax List (which shows 26 acres transferred to Edwin Motley).
This entry repeated annually through 1809, at which time (upon the death of Edwin), the land began to appear in **Elizabeth Motley's** name.
We haven't searched for her on subsequent LTLs.

1808 – Edwin Motley wrote his will in K&Q Co VA on 5 Oct 1808, with a codicil filed 6 Oct 1808, leaving his estate to his wife and children. It was proved in K&Q Co Court on 3 May 1809. Witnesses included Walker Kidd and John Kidd.[42]

---

[39] *A History of Caroline County, Virginia; from its formation in 1727 to 1924*, by Marshall Wingfield, Regional Publishing Company, 1969, p. 70.
[40] *Virginia County Records, Volume VII*, edited by William Armstrong Crozier, Genealogical Publishing Co, 1971, p 100: Marriage Bonds of Caroline Co, VA.
[41] *Caroline County, Virginia Court Records, 1742-1833, and Marriages, 1787-1833*, by William Lindsay Hopkins, Richmond, VA, 1990, p. 82.
[42] A transcription of this will is posted on Ancestry.com, and an image of the transcription is in our K&Q Shared Folder. The will itself is on-line at the Library of Virginia web site, at http://www.virginiamemory.com/collections/lost and search on Motley.

1810 – **Elizabeth Motley** is on the 1810 federal census in K&Q Co with 2 WM under 10, 3 WM 10-15, 1 WM 16-25, 2 WF under 10, 1 WF 16-25, 1 WF 26-44, and 3 slaves.

1820 – On the federal census in Drysdale Parish of K&Q:
Elizabeth Motley: 3WM 16-25; 2WF 10-15 & 1 >44. Forty Slaves (8M<14, 3 14-25, 3 26-44 & 1>44; 10F<14, 8 14-25, 5 26-44 & 2>44. Eighteen people engaged in agriculture.

1830 – On the federal census in K&Q:
Elizabeth Motley: 1WM 5-9 & 1 30-39; 1WF 50-59. Thirty-five slaves (8M<10, 3 10-23, 3 24-35, 3 36-54 & 1 55-99; 8F<10, 3 10-23; 2 24-35, & 4 36-54.

<u>ELIZABETH KIDD MOTLEY BAGBY</u>, the daughter of John Kidd Sr.(3) of K&Q and his wife Ann.
Born abt. 1799
Married first Andrew Motley, by whom she had three children before 1838, when her sister Ann Kidd's will was written: Ann Elizabeth Motley, Mary Frances Motley, and Andrewetta Motley.
 Married second John Bagby and had one child Virginia Bagby by 1838 when her sister Ann's will was written.
Died before 1880

Not dated – In *King and Queen County, Virginia,* by Rev. Alfred Bagby, 1908, p.366, in a section titled "Fragments", Bagby names "Kidd. – John Kidd Sr., lived near Munday's Bridge. Children: John, Mary (Bagby), **Elizabeth (Motley and Bagby)**, John Jr., the father of John B. Kidd."[43]

1838 – Ann Kidd of K&Q County wrote her will, dated 20 May 1838. In it, she named the children of her two sisters, Elizabeth and Mary Ann, and any unborn children, as her heirs.[44]
At the time the will was written, Elizabeth's name was **Elizabeth Bagby**, and she had four daughters Ann Elizabeth Motley, Mary Frances Motley and Andrewetta Motley, and Virginia Bagby. Mary Ann Bagby's[45] children were John Richard Bagby, Ann Elizabeth Bagby, and an unborn child at the writing of Ann Kidd's will, but who was subsequently named Travis Bagby (apparently after his father and Mary Ann's husband, since Mr. Travis Bagby, "my brother-in-law," was named Ann Kidd's executor).
Her will also bequeaths $300 to "Mr. Kidd" for caring for her while she was sick, but doesn't record his given name. Her will was admitted into court in October 1838.[46]

---

[43] *King and Queen County, Virginia,* by Rev. Alfred Bagby, Regional Publishing Co., Baltimore, MD, 1973. (The original book was published in 1908.) This book is available online in the catalog at Familysearch.org and Ancestry.com.

[44] Lost Records Localities Digital Collection, King and Queen County, Kidd, Ann will, 1838. Library of Virginia, Richmond, VA 23219. This will can be seen online at http://www.virginiamemory.com/collections/lost and then searching on "Kidd."

[45] Mary A. Bagby died 17 Oct 1874 in Caroline Co., VA at the age of 64, according to Virginia Deaths and Burials, 1853-1917 at Ancestry.com. Her death record lists her spouse as Travis Bagby, and names her parents as "John and Ann Kidd" (citing FHL #2056976).

[46] King & Queen Chancery Cause 1840-001, online at: http://www.lva.virginia.gov/chancery/case_detail.asp?CFN=097-1840-001 . An abstract of this estate record is available from RK (now stored in the K&Q shared folder). This will and chancery suit also cited in *Index to Virginia Estates, 1800-1865*, vol. 10, compiled by Wesley E. Pippenger, published by Virginia Genealogical Society, 2010.

1839 – On 8 Nov 1839, a suit in Chancery court was heard in K&Q Co for the division of the estate of Ann Kidd. The purpose of the suit was to divide the estate between the children of Ann's sisters Elizabeth and Mary Ann, to establish the inheritance of Travis, the youngest child of Mary Ann Kidd Bagby (she was pregnant at the time of her sister Ann's death), and to make a division of Ann Kidd's slaves.

In a Court held for K&Q County on Friday 8 Nov 1839:
Ann Elizabeth Motley, Mary Frances Motley, Andrewetta Motley and Virginia Bagby, children of **Elizabeth Bagby**; John Richard Bagby, Ann Elizabeth Bagby and Travis Bagby, children of Mary Ann Bagby, all of whom are infants under the age of twenty one years, by John Bagby their next friend, Pltfs.
against
Travis Bagby Executor of Ann Kidd, deceased, Deft. } In Chancery

This cause came on this day by consent of parties to be heard upon the bill and answer, and the will of Ann Kidd filed as [one?] exhibit in the cause and was argued by counsel, upon consideration whereof the Court being of the opinion that the devises or bequests contained in the said will to the future children of Testatrix' two sisters, **Elizabeth Bagby** and Mary Ann Bagby who was *in ventre sa mere*[47] at the death of the said Testatrix

and that the estate devised or bequeathed by the said Testatrix to the children which her said sisters then had and might thereafter have vested in the children which the Testatrix's said sisters had living at the time of her death and in the said infant *in ventre sa mere*, doth therefore adjudge order and decree that the estate of Ann Kidd deceased be divided first into moieties [shares], and that one moiety be divided into four equal parts and the Court doth decree one of said four parts to each of the plaintiffs Elizabeth Motley, Mary Francis Motley, Andrewetta Motley and Virginia Bagby and that James M. Jeffries, John Bagby and Richard Bagby as commissioners for the purpose hereby appointed do fairly value the slaves of the estate of said Ann Kidd and make division of them as herein before ordered and that in said case the said commissioners shall find that the required divisions cannot be made of the slaves in kind, that after advertising the time and place for thirty days at several of the most public places in the neighborhood, they sell one or more of the slaves as the may find necessary upon a credit of six months except as to the expenses of the sale, which they may require in cash, and that they take bonds with good security payable to such of the said parties and for such sums as will affect the required divisions and that the slaves and bonds be delivered to the guardians of those respectively entitled to them and that they report to Court their proceedings herein, and that the Defendant pay over to the guardians of the said **Elizabeth Bagby's** children their respective proportions of the funds in his hands. As to the other moiety of the estate, the use thereof being bequeathed by the Testatrix to the Defendant for the term of five years, the Court doth not make any order in relation thereto at this time, and this cause is retained for future proceedings. The Court doth further order that the effect of this decree be so far suspended, that the parties or their guardians shall not be entitled to receive their portions of the estate until the Defendant shall be properly indemnified by refunding bonds if he require it. The Court doth further adjudge, order and

____

[47] A French law term meaning "in the womb of its mother." Mary Ann was pregnant when her sister Ann died.

decree that the Defendant as Exer. of said Ann Kidd do pay the costs of this suit.[48] [49]

1841 – In a Court held for K&Q Co on 5 May 1841.
Ann Elizabeth Motley, Mary Francis Motley, Andrewetta Motley and Virginia Bagby children of **Elizabeth Bagby**; John Richard Bagby, Ann Elizabeth Bagby and Travis Bagby, children of Mary Ann Bagby, all of whom are infants under the age of twenty one years by John Bagby their next friend, Plts.
against
Travis Bagby, executor of Ann Kidd, dec'd., Deft } In Chancery
This cause came on this day to be again heard on the papers formerly Read and the report of Commissioners having been returned more than one month and no exception having been taken thereto, it is ordered that the same be confirmed.[50]

1850 – on federal census in St. Stephen's Parish, K&Q Co., VA, p. 202A, HH 863:
Bagby, John 58MW grain merchant $8000 VA
   " , **Elizabeth** 51WF VA
   " , John Robert 24MW clerk VA [note: chancery suit names him as John Richard]
   " , Alfred 22MW "none" (no occupation) VA
   " , Martha A. 18FW VA
   " , Mary Ellen 15FW VA attended school within the year
   " , George Thomas 14MW VA attended school within the year
   " , Virginia 11FW VA attended school within the year
   " , Edward 8MW VA attended school within the year
   " , Susan E. 5FW VA

1860 – on federal census in Stevensville P.O. district, K&Q Co., VA, p. 17, HH 135 (mis-indexed as BAGLEY):
Bagby, John 68MW farmer $18,750/27,970 VA
   " , **Elizabeth** 61FW VA
   " , Martha H. 28FW VA
   " , Virginia 21FW VA
   " , Edward 18MW VA attended school within the year
   " , Susan 16FW VA attended school within the year

1870 – on the federal census in Stevensville twp., K&Q Co., VA, Little Plymouth P.O., p. 482, HH 475/480:
Bagby, John 78MW farmer $6000/2000 VA
   " , **Elizabeth** 71FW keeping house VA
   " , Susan 25FW at home VA
Gresham, Alfred 8MW at home VA
Willmore, Lawrence 17MW works on farm VA cannot write

---

[48] King & Queen Chancery Cause 1840-001, online at:
http://www.lva.virginia.gov/chancery/case_detail.asp?CFN=097-1840-001 . An abstract of this estate record is available from RK (now stored in the K&Q shared folder). This will and chancery suit also cited in *Index to Virginia Estates, 1800-1865*, vol. 10, compiled by Wesley E. Pippenger, published by Virginia Genealogical Society, 2010.
[49] King & Queen Co. Order Book, 1831-1851 (LoV reel #8), reviewed by RK July 24, 2018, p. 89. Scanned images available from the authors.
[50] King & Queen Co. Order Book, 1831-1851 (LoV reel #8), reviewed by RK July 24, 2018, p. 107. Scanned image available upon request.

Roane, Nannie 25FB domestic servant VA cannot read or write
Scott, Frances 15FB domestic servant VA cannot read or write
Roy, Franklin 16MB works on farm VA cannot read or write

1880 – Elizabeth is dead before the census date in 1880, and John Bagby is on the 1880 census with daughter Susan still living in his household.

1880 – **Elizabeth Bagby** died of heart disease on 14 March 1880 in K&Q Co VA, at the age of 81 years, 11 months, 3 days.[51] According to this citation, she was born in King William County, which is incorrect, because she would have been born in K&Q Co. The same unsourced records gives John Bagby's death date as 27 June 1880 in K&Q Co VA. The informant for both records was John R. Bagby.

ELIZABETH KIDDs, two free Black females in 1833

On 4 March 1833, an Act of General Assembly was passed "making appropriations for the removal of free persons of color" to the western coast of Africa and established a board of commissioners charged with carrying out the provisions of the act. Localities were required to report to the board regarding their ability to find free blacks who were willing to relocate to Liberia, though many were unable to find people willing or able to do so. One such list was compiled for King & Queen County. This list contains well over 300 names, 26 of whom had the surname of Kidd; it notes the occupation for some and lists their place of residence. See Appendix Two for the full list.[52]

Both **Elizabeth Kidds** were listed on page 6 of this list. The first Elizabeth Kidd was living on Paul Philpot's land, along with Maria, Sarah, Polly, and James Kidd. This may indicate they were a family in the same household. The second Elizabeth Kidd was living on Henry Ware's land; no other Kidds were listed at this location.

Elmira Kidd and **Esperella Kidd**, below, were listed on page 8 of this list, each noted as living "on own land."

ELMIRA KIDD, a free black female in 1833 – See above.

ESPERELLA KIDD, a free black female in 1833 – see above.

FANNY KIDD – only one record found to date for Fanny Kidd in K&Q Co:

1788 – **Fanny Kidd** appears on the membership list (p. 10 of the minute book) for Upper King and Queen Baptist Church, listed as "Dismist." Directly below Fanny Kidd's name appears that of Molley Kidd, listed as "Dismist." Other Kidd individuals mentioned in these church records are Edmund Kidd and William Kidd, Sr. and William Kidd Jr."[53]

---

[51] Virginia Deaths and Burials Index, 1853-1917, at Ancestry.com, citing FHL #2048575, viewable online via familysearch.org at FHL#2048575, image 352 of 373.

[52] Virginia. Auditor of Public Accounts (1776-1928). Free blacks records, 1833-1863. APA 757 1082990_0007_0004_0001_0011 Library of Virginia. This information can be found at "Virginia Untold: The African American Narrative," http://www.virginiamemory.com/collections/aan/.

[53] *Upper King and Queen Baptist Church Records, King and Queen County, 1774-1788*, transcribed by Richard Slatten and Edgar MacDonald, published in Virginia Genealogical Society *Quarterly*, vol. 30, no. 1, p. 64, February 1992.

FRANCES KIDD, a free black female in 1833

On 4 March 1833, an Act of General Assembly was passed "making appropriations for the removal of free persons of color" to the western coast of Africa and established a board of commissioners charged with carrying out the provisions of the act. Localities were required to report to the board regarding their ability to find free blacks who were willing to relocate to Liberia, though many were unable to find people willing or able to do so. One such list was compiled for King & Queen County. This list contains well over 300 names, 26 of whom had the surname of Kidd; it notes the occupation for some and lists their place of residence. See Appendix Two for the full list.[54]

Frances Kidd's name appears on page 8 of this list. Her entry states that she lives on her own land; her occupation was left blank.

FRANK KIDD, a free Black farmer

1813-1826 – In 1813, free Negroes with the surname of Kidd appear for the first time on the K&Q PPTLs. In this year, eleven individuals, 10 males and one female, are found on one of the two tax lists. A **Frank Kidd** was one of those listed. He subsequently appeared on these tax lists intermittently through 1826, but not thereafter, despite the fact he was still listed as living in K&Q in 1833.

YEAR	TAXPAYER	WT	B>16	B 12 -16	H	Cows	COMMENTS
1813	Frank FN	1	0	0	0		Faulkner's list."free Negro"
1814	Frank FN	0	0	0	0		Fleet's list
1816	Frank FN	0	0	0	0		Francis Row's L
1818	Frank FN	X	X	X	X		separate list

YEAR	DATE	TAXPAYER	WMT	B>16	B 12-16	H	COMMENTS
1826	-	Frank FN	x	X	x	x	separate list (57 in all)

1833 – On 4 March 1833, an Act of General Assembly was passed "making appropriations for the removal of free persons of color" to the western coast of Africa and established a board of commissioners charged with carrying out the provisions of the act. Localities were required to report to the board regarding their ability to find free blacks who were willing to relocate to Liberia, though many were unable to find people willing or able to do so. One such list was compiled for King & Queen County. This list contains well over 300 names, 26 of

---

[54] Virginia. Auditor of Public Accounts (1776-1928). Free blacks records, 1833-1863. APA 757 1082990_0007_0004_0001_0011 Library of Virginia. This information can be found at "Virginia Untold: The African American Narrative," http://www.virginiamemory.com/collections/aan/.

whom had the surname of Kidd; it notes the occupation for some and lists their place of residence. See Appendix Two for the full list.[55] **Frank Kidd's** name appears on page 8 of this list; it lists his occupation as "farmer" and states that he lived on his own land. Also on this list is a Hannah Williams (see below), whose place of abode is listed as "at **Frank Kidd's**."

It is possible that this Frank Kidd was among the slaves of John Kidd (1). We base this upon the K&Q PPTLs for this John Kidd between 1783 and 1786 in the table below. The names of at least six of the slaves of John Kidd (1) on the 1783-1786 PPTLs match those individuals who appear as free Negroes in the 1813 PPTLs, some 30 years later; **Frank**, Hannah, Humphrey, James, Sally (variously listed as Sally, Sall and Sarah) and Sam Kidd appear on both lists. And John's slave named Will *could* be the same individual as the free Negro Billy Kidd on the 1813 PPTL. Moreover, of these, all but James and Hannah were under the age of 16 in 1783-1786. While the gap of 30 years and the fact that there may have been other slaves with these given names must be considered, it is possible that John, his wife Lucy, or one of their heirs freed their slaves.

YEAR	TAXPAYER	WT	B>16	B<16	H	Cattle	COMMENTS
1782	John	1	4	7	3	17	slaves not named
1783	John	1	3	6	4	15	8 others listed by name: Lucy,[56] James, Molley, Hannah, Sally, Sam, **Frank**, & Will; only 3 over 16. "2 White Souls"
1784	John	1	3	5	3	15	8 named slaves: James, Molley, Hannah, >16; Humphrey, Sall, **Frank**, Tom & Will <16.
1785	John	1	3	5	3	17	Slaves James, Milly, Hannah, Humphrey, Sarah, Peter, **Frank** & Sam
1786	John	1	4	5	2	16	Slaves James, Humphrey, Hannah, Milly, Peter, Sary, **Frank**, Sam, Will
1787	John	1	5	4	2	15	slaves not named in 1787

[55] Virginia. Auditor of Public Accounts (1776-1928). Free blacks records, 1833-1863. APA 757 1082990_0007_0004_0001_0011 Library of Virginia. This information can be found at "Virginia Untold: The African American Narrative," http://www.virginiamemory.com/collections/aan/.

[56] This particular entry is perplexing because of a column heading - # of White Souls- that occurs in this single year, and which listed 2 white souls for John Kidd. We know from other records that his wife's given name was Lucy, and we believe that she is the Lucy in this record, and the second white tithe, in addition to John.

GEORGE KIDD, a free black male in 1833

1833 -- On 4 March 1833, an Act of General Assembly was passed "making appropriations for the removal of free persons of color" to the western coast of Africa and established a board of commissioners charged with carrying out the provisions of the act. Localities were required to report to the board regarding their ability to find free blacks who were willing to relocate to Liberia, though many were unable to find people willing or able to do so. One such list was compiled for King & Queen County. This list contains well over 300 names, 26 of whom had the surname of Kidd; it notes the occupation for some and lists their place of residence. See Appendix Two for the full list.[57]

George Kidd's name appears on page 8 of this list. It left his occupation blank, and states that he lived upon his own land.

HANNAH KIDD (possibly Hannah Williams), a free Black female and head of household, listed as owning slaves.

1830 – **Hannah Kidd** (mis-indexed as Kedd at Ancestry.com) appears on the federal census for K&Q Co as head of a free black household, p 307:

1 free male 55-99, 1 free female 10-23, **1 free female 55-99**, 1 slave M 55-99, total free colored persons 3, total slaves 1. One person in the household is blind.

This household is listed next to Samuel Kidd, Sally Kidd, and Polly Kidd, all free black heads of households in 1830.

1833 – A **Hannah Williams** appears on a list of free black individuals living in K&Q Co. This may be the Hannah Kidd found in 1830.
Her entry states that her place of abode was "Frank Kidd's;" her occupation was left blank. See Appendix Two for the full list.[58]

It is possible that this Hannah, and Frank Kidd, were among the slaves of John Kidd (1). We base this upon the K&Q PPTLs for this John Kidd between 1783 and 1786 in the table below. The names of at least six of the slaves of John Kidd (1) on the 1783-1786 PPTLs match those individuals who appear as free Negroes in the 1813 PPTLs, some 30 years later; Frank, **Hannah**, Humphrey, James, Sally (variously listed as Sally, Sall and Sarah) and Sam Kidd appear on both lists. And John's slave named Will *could* be the same individual as the free Negro Billy Kidd on the 1813 PPTL. Moreover, of these, all but James and Hannah were under the age of 16 in 1783-1786. While the gap of 30 years and the fact that there may have been other slaves with these given names must be considered, it is possible that John, his wife Lucy, or one of their heirs freed their slaves.

YEAR	TAXPAYER	WT	B>16	B<16	H	Cattle	COMMENTS
1782	John	1	4	7	3	17	slaves not named

---

[57] Virginia. Auditor of Public Accounts (1776-1928). Free blacks records, 1833-1863. APA 757 1082990_0007_0004_0001_0011 Library of Virginia. This information can be found at "Virginia Untold: The African American Narrative," http://www.virginiamemory.com/collections/aan/.
[58] Ibid.

1783	John	1	3	6	4	15	8 others listed by name: Lucy,[59] James, Molley, **Hannah**, Sally, Sam, Frank, & Will; only 3 over 16. "<u>2 White Souls</u>"
1784	John	1	3	5	3	15	8 named slaves: James, Molley, **Hannah**, >16; Humphrey, Sall, Frank, Tom & Will <16.
1785	John	1	3	5	3	17	Slaves James, Milly, **Hannah**, Humphrey, Sarah, Peter, Frank & Sam
1786	John	1	4	5	2	16	Slaves James, Humphrey, **Hannah**, Milly, Peter, Sary, Frank, Sam, Will
1787	John	1	5	4	2	15	slaves not named in 1787 or therafter

HARRIET KIDD WALTON, sister of Nancy S. Kidd and of Polly Kidd Brown, and wife of Isaac Walton. She may not have lived in K&Q.

1835 – In a Court held for K&Q Co on 4 November 1835:[60]

Nancy S. Kidd,[61] Plt vs. Thos. F. Spencer in his own right and as Admr. of Thomas Spencer & also as Admr. of John Spencer; Francis Row, Sheriff of K&Q County & (illegible) Admr of Meacham Spencer; Elvin Brown & **Polly his wife who was Polly Kidd** and Isaac Wharton [Walton] & **Harriett his wife who was Harriett Kidd**, Defts.

The Defts **Elvin Browne and Polly his wife** who are now residents of this state and against whom the Plt appears to have provided(?) in the mode proscribed by Law against absent defendants still failing to appear and answer, and it appearing that the subpoena in this cause has been served more than four months upon the Defts **Isaac Walton**[62] **& Harriet his wife** & they still failing to appear and answer the Bill is taken for Confessed as to them & thereupon this Cause coming on to be heard upon the Bill, answer of the defendant Thomas F. Spencer and the exhibit was argued by Counsel upon consideration whereof & the Plt. waiving at this time any claim to a Decree for any part of Mecham Spencer's proportion of the said balance of $934.92 but without prejudice to its apertion(?) hereafter by Consent of parties it is adjudged, ordered and decreed that the defendant Thos. F. Spencer admr. of

---

[59] This particular entry is perplexing because of a column heading - # of White Souls- that occurs in this single year, and which listed 2 white souls for John Kidd. We know from other records that his wife's given name was Lucy, and we believe that she is the Lucy in this record, and the second white tithe, in addition to John.

[60] Circuit Superior Court of Law and Chancery, Order Books: Order Book, 1831-1851, LoV ILL reel 2, FHL #32114 – restricted access. Pp. 52-53. Digital images available upon request.

[61] At this time the identity of this woman is unknown. Note that Benjamin Kidd's first wife was an Ann Spencer. There is only one other mention of Spencer in this BD, in which John(1) Kidd was an adjoining neighbor. – RK

[62] The name is indeed written WHARTON in the title, but WALTON in the body of the record.)

John Spencer out of the assets of the said John Spencer in his hands, if so much he have, if not out of his own proper goods & chattels pay to the plaintiff Nancy S. Kidd the sum of $101.87 with interest thereon at the rate of six per centum per annum from the 1ˢᵗ day of January 1827 until paid and her costs expended in the prosecution of this suit upon the said **Nancy S. Kidd** or some person for his(?) executing to the said Thomas F. Spencer, admr. of John Spencer a refunding bond with good security conditioned(?) according to Law. But this decree is without prejudice to any claim which the aid Plaintiff may hereafter assert to a proportion of Mecham Spencer's part of the estate of John Spencer or to any claim which the Defts. **Elvin Brown & Polly his wife and Isaac Walton & Harriett his wife** may assert to their portions of John or Mecham Spencer's Estate.

HENRY KIDD (1) of Middlesex Co VA, the son of Benjamin and Jane Kidd

Henry5 (Benjamin4, Benjamin3, William2, Thomas1) Kidd
Born by 1766, most likely in Middlesex Co.
Married Catherine Seward in MSX in 1803
Spent most of his life in MSX, but left some records in K&Q, listed below.
Died testate in 1803 in MSX
See his section in our Middlesex compilation at www.kiddroots.org for more details about his life and his records.

1784 – a **Henry Kidd** appears on the K&Q PPTL in the Second Hundred (tax district) this one year.[63] His entry is followed by the annotation "(prop)," suggesting that he's the property owner, but not a resident of this county. This entry names his overseer, Jno. Brown, and his four taxable slaves – Charles, George, Peter and Billy.
Henry Kidd is not found on these tax lists in subsequent years.
A William Kidd also appears on this PPTL this one year only. His relationship, if any, to Henry is unknown at this time.
See the Figure below.

---

[63] This tax "district" was most likely in the upper portion of K&Q, in the middle of St. Stephens Parish.

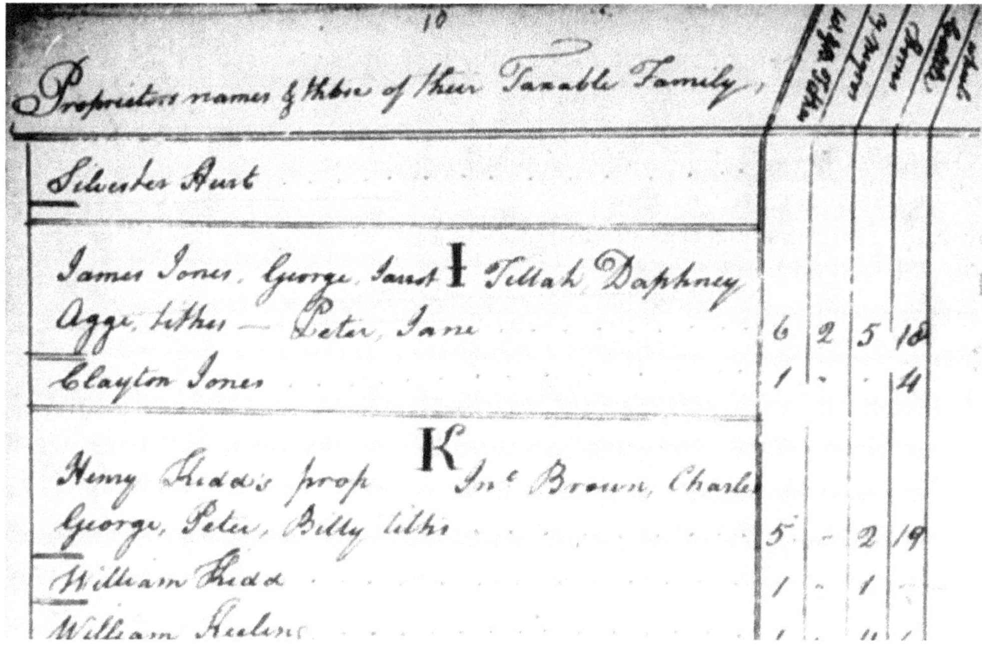

FIGURE: 1784 K&Q PPTL entries for Henry and William Kidd.[64] The "Names" column heading for this year reads, "Proprietors' Names & those of their taxable family." The other column headings are W & B tithes/Y(oung) Negroes/Horses/ Cattle/Wheels.

1796-1802 – a **Henry Kidd** again appears on the K&Q PPTLs in 1796, charged with no white tithes. He then appears annually through 1802, each year charged with one white tithe, as depicted on the Table below:

YEAR	TAXPAYER	WT	B>16	B 12 -16	H	COMMENTS
1796	Henry	0	1	0	0	Beverly Roy's list
1797	Henry	1	1	0	2	Beverly Roy's list
1798	Henry	1	0	0	1	Beverly Roy's list
1799	Henry	1	0	0	2	Beverly Roy's list
1800	Henry	1	1	0	3	Beverly Roy's list
1801	Henry	1	1	0	2	Wm Fleet's list
1802	Henry	1	1	0	2	Shackelford's list

In 1803, he drops from these PPTLs , and does not reappear.

This is **Henry Kidd** of Middlesex Co VA, who does not appear in MSX Co PPTLs in the years in which he appears on K&Q Co PPTLs. He died in 1803 in Middlesex County, VA. His K&Q lands were ordered to be sold at his death to pay debts of his estate, and were sold before 1810, per his MSX Co estate accts. We don't know the acreage of this land, but it

---

[64] Retrieved from Binnsgenealogy.com, Personal Property Tax Lists, King and Queen County, Virginia, 1782-1803, 1784, image 8.

sold for £81, 11 shillings, 1 pence.
See the Middlesex County compilation for more information on this Henry Kidd.

HENRY KIDD (2), father of John Kidd(2) in this compilation.
Birth date and place are unknown.
Lived in the southeastern part of K&Q Co
Died by 1802, most likely in K&Q

1800, 1801 – a **Henry Kidd** first appears in the K&Q LTLs in 1800, taxed for 81½ acres. This listing repeats in 1801.

1802, 1803 – **Henry Kidd's** entry in the K&Q LTLs for 1802 is for his estate, and he has died in the past 12 months. His estate is taxed on the same 81½ acres again in 1803, after which it drops from the LTLs.

1804 – The year that **Henry Kidd's** estate drops from the LTLs, a **John Kidd** appears for the first time, taxed on 81½ acres, providing evidence that this John was Henry's eldest son. The location of this land is recorded as 9 mile SE of the K&Q Courthouse in 1815.   See John(2) Kidd section.

HENRY KIDD (3) – in K&Q Co in 1830

1830 – on the federal census in K&Q Co VA, p. 288, line 12 (next door is Ann Kidd):
Henry Kidd – 1M 20-29 and 1 F 15-19; one male slave under 10.

HENRY KIDD (unplaced)

Circa 1783 – a **Henry Kidd** and a John Kidd appear on "Miss Anne Walker Reddy's list of persons rendering Revolutionary Service, Military and Non-military, from King and Queen County."[65]
This statement is verified by K&Q Co Court records for claims submitted for livestock, supplies, and provisions supplied to the County or to the Continental Army during the Revolutionary War, where Henry Kidd's name appears among those granted certificates: On a list of certificates delivered by Robert Hill, commissioner for K&Q County for provisions received for the use of the army… this list includes "**Henry Kidd**, by hands Jno. Draper, 5 barrels corn."[66]

HUMPHREY KIDD, a free Black farmer, 1813-1833

1813-1826 – A Humphrey Kidd appears intermittently on the PPTLs for K&Q County, beginning in 1813, and continuing until 1826, but not thereafter.
In 1816 (this one year only), two males by this name are listed.

---

[65] *Virginia Colonial Abstracts*, volume 5, by Beverley Fleet, p. 15.
[66] *Virginia Revolutionary Claims*, compiled and transcribed by Janice L. Abercrombie and Richard Slatten, Iberian Publishing Co., Athens, GA, 1992 (three volumes in 1, 1113 pages), p. 553.

1813	Humphrey Kidd	"free Negro"
1814	Humphrey Kidd	"free Negro"
1816	Humphrey Kidd	"free Negro"
1816	Humphrey Kidd Sr.	"free Negro"
1817	Humphrey Kidd	"free Negro"
1818	Humphrey Kidd	"free Negro"
1820	Humphrey Kidd	"free Negro"
1826	Humphrey Kidd	"free Negro"

1820, 1830 – We do not find him on the 1820 or the 1830 federal census in K&Q County.

1833 – **Humphrey Kidd** appears on a list of free black individuals living in K&Q Co (see Appendix Two for the full list); he is listed on page 6, living on George Moore's land."[67]

It is possible that this Humphrey Kidd was among the slaves of John Kidd (1). We base this upon the K&Q PPTLs for this John Kidd between 1783 and 1786 in the table below. The names of at least six of the slaves of John Kidd (1) on the 1783-1786 PPTLs match those individuals who appear as free Negroes in the 1813 PPTLs, some 30 years later; Frank, Hannah, **Humphrey**, James, Sally (variously listed as Sally, Sall and Sarah) and Sam Kidd appear on both lists. And John's slave named Will *could* be the same individual as the free Negro Billy Kidd on the 1813 PPTL. Moreover, of these, all but James and Hannah were under the age of 16 in 1783-1786. While the gap of 30 years and the fact that there may have been other slaves with these given names must be considered, it is possible that John, his wife Lucy, or one of their heirs freed their slaves.

YEAR	TAXPAYER	WT	B>16	B<16	H	Cattle	COMMENTS
1782	John	1	4	7	3	17	slaves not named
1783	John	1	3	6	4	15	8 others listed by name: Lucy,[68] James, Molley, Hannah, Sally, Sam, Frank, & Will; only 3 over 16. "2 White Souls"

---

[67] Virginia. Auditor of Public Accounts (1776-1928). Free blacks records, 1833-1863. APA 757 1082990_0007_0004_0001_0011 Library of Virginia. This information can be found at "Virginia Untold: The African American Narrative," http://www.virginiamemory.com/collections/aan/.

[68] This particular entry is perplexing because of a column heading - # of White Souls- that occurs in this single year, and which listed 2 white souls for John Kidd. We know from other records that his wife's given name was Lucy, and we believe that she is the Lucy in this record, and the second white tithe, in addition to John.

1784	John	1	3	5	3	15	8 named slaves: James, Molley, Hannah, >16; **Humphrey**, Sall, Frank, Tom & Will <16.
1785	John	1	3	5	3	17	Slaves James, Milly, Hannah, **Humphrey**, Sarah, Peter, Frank & Sam
1786	John	1	4	5	2	16	Slaves James, **Humphrey**, Hannah, Milly, Peter, Sary, Frank, Sam, Will
1787	John	1	5	4	2	15	slaves not named in 1787

ISAAC KIDD

1792 – An **Isaac Kidd** appears on the annual K&Q PPTLs only in this year, charged with one white male tithe, five slaves and three horses.[69] He's never listed again on these lists through 1855.

JAMES KIDD, in K&Q Co as of 1788 and in 1790s

1788 – In an article abstracting Upper King & Queen Baptist Church records:
1788 **James Kidd** and Betsy Kidd dismist.
Nov (1788) Thomas Kidd and Betsy Kidd dismist.[70] Also appearing in earlier records for this church were Fanny Kidd, Molley Kidd, John Kidd, William Kidd Sr. and William Kidd Jr.
[N.B. The entry for Thomas appears to be a clerical error. We've found no records in this timeframe for a Thomas Kidd].

1791, 1792 – a **James Kidd** appears on the K&Q PPTLs these two years, each time charged with one white male tithe.

1795-1799 – after not appearing on the K&Q PPTLs for several years, **James Kidd** reappears on the 1795 PPTL, and is listed annually through 1799, taxed on one white male tithe, but not thereafter.

We have found no further records for this James Kidd in K&Q.

JAMES KIDD, a free black head of household 1813-1840

1813-1843 – a free Negro named James Kidd appears for the first time on the K&Q PPTLs in 1816, and appears on these tax lists regularly but not annually through 1843, as shown on the Table below:

YEAR	TAXPAYER	NOTATION	COMMENTS
1813	James Kidd	"free Negro"	Dist. Of Benj. Faulkner

---

[69] Found on Binnsgenealogyc.com, K&Q County PPTLs, 1782-1803, tax list 1792B, image 7.
[70] *Magazine of Virginia Genealogy*, volume 52, pages 263-265, 2014.

1814	James Kidd	"free Negro"	Dist. Of John W. Fleet
1818	James Kidd	"free Negro"	List of Francis Row; separate list of "Free Negroes & Mulattos" end of this list.
1820	James Kidd	"free Negro"	List of Francis Row; separate list of "Free Negroes & Mulattos" end of this list.
1826	James Kidd	"free Negro"	A separate list of other FNs found at the end of the main list.
1838	James Kidd	"free Negro"	
1840	James Kidd	"free Negro"	List of John Pollard; with W polls
1841	James Kidd	"free Negro"	List of John Pollard; with W polls
1842	James Kidd	"free Negro"	On separate list at end this year
1843	James Kidd	"free Negro"	On separate list at end this year

1820 – a **James Kidd, fn (for Free Negro)** appears on the federal census in Stratton Major Parish of K&Q Co as head of a free Black family. In this HH are 3 free black males under 14, 4 FBM 14-25, and 2 FBM 26-44; 3 free black females under 14, 2 FBF 14-25, 1 FBF 26-44 and 1 FBF 45 or over.[71] Also on this census is another free black family, that of Samuel Kidd.

1830 – no **James Kidd** is found on the federal census in this year.

1833 – **James Kidd** appears on a list of free black individuals living in K&Q Co, living on Paul Philpot's land, with no occupation listed. Also listed as living on Paul Philpot's land were Maria, Sarah, Polly, and Elizabeth Kidd, with no occupations listed. This may indicate they were a family in the same household. See Appendix Two for the full list.[72]

1840 – a **James Kidd** appears on the federal census in K&Q, a free Black man, age 24-35. He may have been one of the males under 14 in the 1820 HH above. In the James Kidd 1840 household are 3 free black females under 10, 4 FBF between 10-23 and 1 FBF 55-99. Also in the HH is one male slave, age 24-35.[73]

---

[71] Ancestry.com, p. 156A (image 2/16). Names in order of first letter of last name, by parish.

[72] Virginia. Auditor of Public Accounts (1776-1928). Free blacks records, 1833-1863. APA 757 1082990_0007_0004_0001_0011 Library of Virginia. This information can be found at "Virginia Untold: The African American Narrative," http://www.virginiamemory.com/collections/aan/.

[73] On page 115, images 65-66/68 at Ancestry.com.

It is possible that this James Kidd was among the slaves of John Kidd (1). We base this upon the K&Q PPTLs for this John Kidd between 1783 and 1786 in the table below. The names of at least six of the slaves of John Kidd (1) on the 1783-1786 PPTLs match those individuals who appear as free Negroes in the 1813 PPTLs, some 30 years later; Frank, Hannah, Humphrey, **James**, Sally (variously listed as Sally, Sall and Sarah) and Sam Kidd appear on both lists. And John's slave named Will *could* be the same individual as the free Negro Billy Kidd on the 1813 PPTL. Moreover, of these, all but James and Hannah were under the age of 16 in 1783-1786. While the gap of 30 years and the fact that there may have been other slaves with these given names must be considered, it is possible that John, his wife Lucy, or one of their heirs freed their slaves.

YEAR	TAXPAYER	WT	B>16	B<16	H	Cattle	COMMENTS
1782	John	1	4	7	3	17	slaves not named
1783	John	1	3	6	4	15	8 others listed by name: Lucy,[74] **James**, Molley, Hannah, Sally, Sam, Frank, & Will; only 3 over 16. "<u>2 White Souls</u>"
1784	John	1	3	5	3	15	8 named slaves: **James**, Molley, Hannah, >16; Humphrey, Sall, Frank, Tom & Will <16.
1785	John	1	3	5	3	17	Slaves **James**, Milly, Hannah, Humphrey, Sarah, Peter, Frank & Sam
1786	John	1	4	5	2	16	Slaves **James**, Humphrey, Hannah, Milly, Peter, Sary, **Frank**, Sam, Will
1787	John	1	5	4	2	15	slaves not named in 1787

JINNY KIDD, in K&Q Co as of 1853

1853 – A **Jinny Kidd** appears on the K&Q PPTL in 1853, with no WM tithes in her household. She then drops from these lists (through 1855, the last year we've checked). Her relationship to the other Kidds is not known.

---

[74] This particular entry is perplexing because of a column heading - # of White Souls- that occurs in this single year, and which listed 2 white souls for John Kidd. We know from other records that his wife's given name was Lucy, and we believe that she is the Lucy in this record, and the second white tithe, in addition to John.

JOANNA KIDD, died Jan 1850 in K&Q Co

1850 – A 34-year-old married woman named **Joanna Kidd** died in K&Q Co in January of 1850; the cause of death is difficult to decipher in the record, but appears to say "Child Bed" of 2 days' duration. This probably refers to childbed fever, indicating an infection following the delivery of a child.[75]

JOEL H. KIDD (B 1807, d by Jan 1855), the son of Willis and Lucy ___ Kidd of Caroline Co VA.[76]

Joel H.6 (Willis5, William4, Daniel3, Thomas2, Thomas1) Kidd
Born abt 1807
Found primarily in Essex and Caroline Cos. Appears in K&Q Co tax lists only in the 1840s.
Died in Essex County in 1855.

Most of the records for Joel H. Kidd are found in Essex and Caroline Cos. Please see these county compilations at www.kiddroots.org. There is only one man named Joel Kidd in this timeframe, so we believe these records are for the same man.

1841 – **Joel Kidd** first appears on the annual PPTL in **K&Q Co** in this year, with 1 white male tithe, 4 taxable slaves, 3 horses and a gig worth $50.

1842-1846 – **Joel Kidd** continues to appear annually on the **K&Q PPTLs**, each year with 1 white male tithe, then drops from the lists.

1842-1848 – **Joel H. Kidd** appears on the **K&Q LTLs** in 1842 (he might have appeared in 1841, but the K page for that year's LTL is missing from the microfilm). In 1842, he's taxed for 209 acres "adj. Samuel Gresham, 28 miles NW of the courthouse." This is in the northern parish, and in the vicinity of the John Kidd households on or near the Mattapony River. This same entry repeats through 1848, after which **Joel H. Kidd** drops from the K&Q LTLs. Not noted on LTLs what became of his land.

See his section in our Essex County, Virginia compilation on our website, www.kiddroots.org, for more information on **Joel H. Kidd**.

JOHN KIDD(s)

There are at least 5 white John Kidds and two free Black John Kidds living in King & Queen County between 1763 and 1855, as seen below:

John Kidd (1) on LTLs starting in 1782, died by 1800. Estate listed on LTLs through 1812, in same District as those living in the southeastern part of county.

John Kidd (2) (aka John Kidd Junr in some K&Q records**),** living 9 mi SE of CH, inherits or purchases Henry Kidd's 81½ acre tract 9 miles SE of the Courthouse circa 1804; appears on LTLs starting in 1804; named as John Kidd Jr. starting in 1821 when the LTL tax districts

---

[75] The 1850 federal census mortality schedule for K&Q Co., available online at Familysearch.org.

[76] We have found no direct evidence that proves he was the son of Willis & Lucy __ Kidd, but this seems most likely to us. Other trees list his parents as William Kidd and his wife, Mary Halbert, but in fact these two were the parents of the elder Joel Kidd (above), and of Willis Kidd. Joel H. Kidd DID name one of his sons Henry Willis Kidd, and this is supportive, but not conclusive.

are combined into one district (to distinguish him from the older man known as John Kidd Sr., of Lumpkin and Co.); dies by 1833, when his estate is listed on the LTLs as John Kidd Junr Estate; drops from LTLs in 1836.

John Kidd (3) (aka John Kidd Sr., or John Kidd of Lumpkin and Co), living 30 miles NW of the Courthouse, on Mattapony River; appears on LTLs starting in 1809; dies by 1838 (estate listed as John Kidd Estate in 1839 and 1840, 1841 list missing, dropped from list by 1842).

John Kidd (4) (aka John Kidd Junr, Estate), son of John Kidd Sr. (John3), whose estate is found on K&Q LTLs only for three years in 1837-1839, so has died by 1837; land is at 22 mi NW of CH close to land of John Kidd Sr.

John Kidd (5), whose land lies 18 mi E of the CH, who has died by 1819 when his estate is listed on the LTLs. From 1819 through 1827, the LTL entries reads John Kidd Estate (Free Negros or F.N.), which may mean that Free Negros are living on the John Kidd estate, though his association with these families is not known. Starting in 1828, the Estate is listed as John Kidd Estate (with no Free Negros identifier) and continues through 1856, dropping from the list in 1857.

John Kidds, two free Negroes who appear in K&Q, both in 1833, and one in two other records, 1826 and 1842.

JOHN KIDD (1), son of Henry Kidd, so named in Henry's Essex Co VA will written in 1785. Born before 1742[77]
This John Kidd is the earliest Kidd man found in surviving K&Q records.[78]
When he and his siblings sold his father's land in 1794, he was listed as of King and Queen Co
Died in K&Q abt. 1800; his wife Lucy survived him.

1763-1771 – " At a Vestry held for Stratton Major Parish at the Upper Church on Tuesday the 8th day of November 1763 .....to **John Kidd** for keeping Mildred Evans 15 months, 1000# tobacco." [79] It's not clear from the vestry book whether this is payment in advance for housing an orphan or elderly person, or if this is payment for housing her in the past. Subsequent entries through 1771 show that he continued to provide for Mildred Evans through October 1771, when the Vestry "orders that **John Kidd** receive 400# tobacco for keeping Mildred Evans two years."[80]

1767 – Vestry records of Stratton Major Parish in K&Q Co show that in November 1767, pew N4 of the church was allotted to "the wife of **John Kidd**," among others.[81] Having a church pew was a sign of wealth and status in the colonial parish.

---

[77] Judging from the citations in the Stratton Major Parish Vestry Book.
[78] However, the Stratton Major Parish Vestry Book, which covers the southern part of the county, is the only source that has Kidd records before the 1770s.
[79] *The Vestry Book of Stratton Major Parish, King and Queen County, Virginia, 1729-1783*, Stratton Major Parish (Va.), Division of Purchase and Printing, 1931, p. 145.
[80] *Ibid*, p. 189.
[81] *Ibid*, p. 170.

1779 – a **John Kidd** appears on an unidentified record in 1779 (Ancestry.com, without documentation, terms this record as a K&Q Co Rent Roll, but there are no known rent rolls for this county in this timeframe.)

1781-1783 – In February 1781, **John Kidd** was appointed a Vestryman of Stratton Major Parish.[82] He continued to serve through 1783 (the last year covered by this vestry book). At a Vestry held for Stratton Major Parish on Saturday, 13 Dec 1783, John Kidd was one of the 8 vestry men present; he was appointed Church Warden for the coming year, along with Richard Anderson.[83]

1782 – On 25 January 1782, **John Kidd** was appointed assistant inspector of Tobacco at Shepherds warehouses in K&Q Co.[84]

In 1782, a Henry Kidd and a **John Kidd** appear on "Miss Anne Walker Reddy's list of persons rendering Revolutionary Service, Military and Non-military, from King and Queen County."[85]
This statement is supported by Gloucester Co Court records for claims submitted for livestock, supplies, provisions, etc. supplied to the County or to the Continental Army during the Revolutionary War:
Gloucester Co Court Booklet. At a court held for Gloucester Co 5 April 1782 for receiving and adjusting claims agreeable to an Act of Assembly for that purpose, the court doth set and estimate: (p. 15) Alexander Roan, 111# bacon, 550# beef (delivered to **John Kidd of K&Q**), £19.13.4.[86]

John Kidd is also found in the K&Q Co Court records for Revolutionary War claims. **Jno. Kidd** received a certificate for providing 5 gallons, 4½ pints brandy, £139.1.3; there are five records in which **John Kidd** was the person certifying the claim of another individual, suggesting that he played an official role.[87]

1782-1787 – PPTL records began in Virginia in 1782. A **John Kidd** appears on the first K&Q Co PPTL and continues to be listed annually through 1799. In these early PPTLs, he is consistently found on the tax list of the Sixth Hundred, a designation that places him in the southern-most area of K&Q. In 1800, the entry lists the **John Kidd estate**; while the writing is not clear, it appears to say Est. (Estate), which matches the 1800 LTLs.]

YEAR	TAXPAYER	WT	B>16	B<16	H	Cattle	COMMENTS
1782	John	1	4	7	3	17	slaves not named
1783	John	1	3	6	4	15	8 others listed by name: Lucy, James, Molley, Hannah, Sally,

[82] Ibid, p. 222.

[83] Ibid, p. 229.

[84] *Journals of the Council of the state of Virginia*, v.3 1781:Dec.1-1786:Nov.29, page 35, viewed online at Hathitrust: https://catalog.hathitrust.org/Record/003081841).

[85] *Virginia Colonial abstracts*, volume 5, by Beverley Fleet, p. 15.

[86] *Virginia Revolutionary Claims*, compiled and transcribed by Janice L. Abercrombie and Richard Slatten, Iberian Publishing Co., Athens, GA, 1992 (three volumes in 1, 1113 pages), p. 393.

[87] *Virginia Revolutionary Claims*, compiled and transcribed by Janice L. Abercrombie and Richard Slatten, Iberian Publishing Co., Athens, GA, 1992 (three volumes in 1, 1113 pages), p. 561.

						Sam, Frank, & Will; only 3 over 16. "2 White Souls"
1784	John	1	3	5	3	15	8 named slaves: James, Molley, Hannah, >16; Humphrey, Sall, Frank, Tom & Will <16.
1785	John	1	3	5	3	17	Slaves James, Milly, Hannah, Humphrey, Sarah, Peter, Frank & Sam
1786	John	1	4	5	2	16	Slaves James, Humphrey, Hannah, Milly, Peter, Sary, Frank, Sam, Will
1787	John	1	5	4	2	15	slaves not named in 1787

Note: The names of at least six of the slaves of **John Kidd (1)** on the 1783-1786 PPTLs match those individuals who appear as free Negroes in the 1813 PPTLs, some 30 years later; Frank, Hannah, Humphrey, James, Sally (variously listed as Sally, Sall and Sarah) and Sam Kidd appear on both lists. And John's slave named Will *could* be the same individual as the free Negro Billy Kidd on the 1813 PPTL. Moreover, of these, all but James and Hannah were under the age of 16 in 1783-1786. While the gap of 30 years and the fact that there may have been other slaves with these given names must be considered, it is possible that John, his wife Lucy, or one of their heirs freed their slaves.

1788-1800 – In 1788, the column heading recording young slaves changed from listing the number of all slaves under 16 to enumerating those between the age of 12-16 (and thus presumably excluding those slaves under 12 years old from taxation).
John Kidd continues to appear on these PPTLs annually through 1799.

YEAR	TAXPAYER	WT	B>16	B 12 -16	H	COMMENTS
1788	John	1	6	0	2	No slaves 12-16
1789	John	1	6	1	2	Wm Fleet's list
1790	John	1	6	0	2	Wm Fleet's list
1791	John	1	5	2	2	Wm Fleet's list
1792	John	1	5	2	1	Wm Fleet's list
1793	John	1	0	0	1	Wm Courtney's list

1793	John	1	6	1	2	Wm Fleet's list
1794	John	1	6	3	2	Wm Fleet's list
1795	John	1	7	1	2	Wm Fleet's list
1796	John	1	7	1	2	Beverly Roy's list
1797	John	1	7	2	2	Beverly Roy's list
1798	John	1	8	0	2	Beverly Roy's list
1799	John	1	8	0	5	Beverly Roy's list
1800	John	0	8	1	4	Beverly Roy's list; John's name followed by "Bin"? [88]

John Kidd apparently was deceased by the spring of 1800 when this tax list was made, because his entry lists no white tithes for this year. The abbreviation following John Kidd's name in 1800 is hard to decipher. It doesn't look like two other common abbreviations (i.e., Dcd. and Est.) that indicate the taxpayer is deceased; another possibility is that it represents 'Emt' or 'Exm,' an abbreviation of Exempt (due to disability or age).

John Kidd then drops from the K&Q PPTLs from 1801 through 1803, and his wife/widow Lucy appears on them in 1801, with the same number of slaves and horses that John had in 1800.

1782, 1787-1813 – **Land Tax Lists** (LTLs) began in Virginia in 1782. A **John Kidd** appears on the first county list in 1782, taxed for 370 acres, and the **John Kidd Estate** first appears in 1800. LTLs for 1783, 1784, and 1786 do not survive, and he is not found on the 1785 and 1790 lists, and was evidently missed. Starting in 1787, he is found each year through 1799. His estate is found beginning in 1800 through 1813:

Year	NAME	Acres	Description	CH	COMMENTS
1782	John Kidd	370			
1783-1786					No records 1783, 1784, 1786 Not found on 1785 list
1787-1789	John Kidd	370 25			- "from Thomas Pierce"
1790					Not found

---

[88] Digital image of the record available upon request.

Year	NAME	Acres	Description	CH	COMMENTS
1791-1792	John Kidd	370 60			- "from Lumpkin & Pierce"
1793-1799	John Kidd	370 60 45			- from Lumpkin & Pierce from Thomas Dillard
1800-1812	John Kidd Estate	370 60 45			
1813	Estate drops from LTLs				Disposition of land not known

1784 – On 18 March 1784, **John Kid** was appointed by the General Assembly of Virginia to be an inspector of tobacco at Shepherds warehouses in King & Queen Co.[89]

1785 – On 1 Nov 1785, **John Kidd** and Richard Bray, tobacco inspectors at Shepherd's Warehouse, filed a petition to the Virginia Legislature for reimbursement. Their petition states that at some point in the night of 6 May 1785 someone did break into Shepherd's Warehouse and make off with two hogsheads of tobacco, one inspected for Ann Dillard and weighing 1085 lb and the other inspected for James Glaspie and weighing 1026 lb. It's not known what action was taken on this petition.[90]

1787 – **John Kidd** appears on the membership list (p. 8 of the Minutes book) for Upper King and Queen Baptist Church on July 6, listed as "Dismist" followed by "Returned." Directly below John Kidd's name appears that of Edmund Kidd, listed as "Dismist."[91] Other Kidd individuals mentioned in these church records are Fanny Kidd, Molley Kidd, William Kidd, Sr. and William Kidd Jr.[92]

1794 – In an Essex Co VA deed dated: 15 Dec 1794, **John Kidd and Lucy, his wife**, of King and Queen County, along with his brother William and sisters Mary and Sarah, sell land inherited from their father Henry Kidd of Essex Co VA:[93]

Grantors: **John Kidd and Lucy his wife}**
      William Kidd   } of King and Queen County
      John Brown and Mary his wife }

---

[89] *Journals of the Council of the state of Virginia*, v.3 1781:Dec.1-1786:Nov.29, page 333, viewed online at Hathitrust: https://catalog.hathitrust.org/Record/003081841).

[90] Legislative Petitions of the General Assembly, 1776-1865, Accession number 36121, Box 163, folder 8

[91] *Upper King and Queen Baptist Church Records, King and Queen County, 1774-1788*, transcribed by Richard Slatten and Edgar MacDonald, published in Virginia Genealogical Society *Quarterly*, vol. 30, no. 1, p. 63, February 1992.

[92] *Magazine of Virginia Genealogy*, volume 30, pp. 63-64.

[93] Essex County (VA) Deed Book 34, p. 91 (also pp 205, 206 and 207), John Kidd et al to Thomas Roane, Abstracted by Nancy Heuser for Sandra Kidd, Oct. 2007. Note: "The deed then had a "p.s. Two graveyards excepted with half an acre of land around the one where the white people are buried and the privilege of carrying any corps to the same."
Pgs. 205, 207 and 207 are the relinquishments of dower by the three women, Lucy Kidd, Mary Brown and Sarah Kidd [the latter the wife of Benjamin Kidd].

Benjamin Kidd and Sarah his wife}   of Caroline County
Grantee: Thomas Roane of Essex County
Consideration: 400 Pounds and one shilling current money
Tract: A Parcel of land in County of Essex and Parish of South Farnham containing 275 acres. Metes and bounds description, mostly referencing distances to certain trees, but did name lines of Haile, Allen and Dix. Included two tracts of land, one containing 124 ½ acres the second 151 acres. Referenced them as "being those tracts of land whereon Henry Kidd lately lived and of which he died seized and which the said John and William Kidd, Mary Brown and Sarah Kidd are entitled to under the last will and testament of the said Henry Kidd."

Signed and sealed:	**Jno Kidd**
	William Kidd
	John Brown
	Benjamin Kidd
Witnesses:	William Wood
	John Allen
	Philemon Purkins
	James Allen
Deed rec.:	15 Dec 1794

1796 – On 2 June, **John Kidd's Company** is listed among the King and Queen militia companies receiving fines; unnamed men in his company were fined a total of 16.50 [type of currency not listed].[94] [Not known for certain this is the same John Kidd, but it is feasible that, as a man of means, he would head a company of militia.]

1799 – **John Kidd** appears on a 1799 list of the Justices of K&Q Co, 1799-1801, abstracted by Beverly Fleet in vol. 15 of his K&Q records. Fleet cites the list as being held at the LOV's Archives Division, in the Executive Papers of Gov. James Monroe, Aug 1801. This was a list of the Gentlemen Justices, filed by Robert Pollard, Clerk of Court, 10 Aug 1801, that would have appeared in the 1801 Order Book, had it survived the fires:

"Agreeable to the foregoing Order I do hereby certify that I have examined the proceedings of the County Court of King and Queen and find that the Magistrates were present on the Court days under their respective names affixed….

"**John Kidd**, 1799 on Aug't 12th, 13th, 14th, 15th; on Septr 9th, 10th; on Novr 14th, 15th, 16th." **John Kidd** appears between the entries for Rich'd Corbin and Thomas Roane, Jr. His name does not appear after 16 Nov, so he may have been deceased by then.[95]

1800-1812 –**John Kidd** died in late 1799 or early 1800; the 1800 K&Q Land Tax List lists his estate for the first time. These entries repeat through 1812, and then drop from the K&Q LTLs. We do not know the disposition of his substantial land holdings, but his wife Lucy survived him (below).

---

[94] *Virginia Colonial Abstracts*, Vol II, citing vol. 27 of Fleet's abstracts of King and Queen Co, pp. 89-90.
[95] *Virginia Colonial Abstracts*, vol. 15, King and Queen County records, pp. 86, 89, by Beverley Fleet.

1801 – **Lucy Kidd,** John Kidd's widow, appears on the K&Q PPTL in 1801, the year after John Kidd drops from these annual PPTLs with no white male tithes in her HH. She has the same number of slaves that John Kidd did in 1800.

YEAR	TAXPAYER	WT	B>16	B 12 -16	H	COMMENTS
1801	Lucy	0	8	1	3	Wm Fleet's list

She drops from the PPTLs in 1802 and does not reappear.

1801 – 16 June 1801, **Essex County** court. **Lucy Kidd,** executrix of **John Kidd, deceased,** Petitioner against Thomas Dix and John Croxton, Defendants} On Petition Defendants though solemnly called failed to appear…Court rules that the petitioner recover of the defendants the sum of £4.5.2, and also her costs…the defendants in mercy, etc…this Judgment is to be discharged by the payment of £1.2 with interest from 1 January 1794 till payment, and her costs.[96]

JOHN KIDD (2), apparent son of Henry Kidd of K&Q Co who died by 1802.
Born bet. 1781-1790[97]
Wife most likely was Jane Baker, and sons William and Robert. Unable to read or write.
Lived 9 miles southeast of the K&Q courthouse in Stratton Major Parish, the southern parish of the county.
Died ca 1832 in K&Q County

1804, ff. – a **John Kidd** first appears on the K&Q **PPTLs** in 1804, and appears annually there through 1825 [missing only in 1813, and likely overlooked].

YEAR	TAXPAYER	WT	B>16	B 12 -16	H	Cows	COMMENTS
1804	John	1	0	1	2		Shackelford's list
1805	John	1	0	0	2		Spencer's list
1806	John	1	1	0	2		Spencer's list
1807	John	2	0	0	1		Spencer's list
1808	No Tax						
1809	John	1	0	0	2		Faulkner's list
1809	John	1	6	0	4		Pollard's list

[In 1809, he is joined on the K&Q PPTLs by a second, wealthier John Kidd. Note that this second John Kidd is in the other tax district of K&Q, in the northwestern portion of the county.] See below for a continuation of these PPTLs.

1804, ff. – a **John Kidd** also appears on the K&Q **LTLs** of 1804, taxed upon 81½ acres. This is the identical amount of land that in 1802 and 1803 was in Henry Kidd's estate, leading us to

---

[96] Essex County Order Book 36, page 154.
[97] Judging from his age categories on the various censuses: 1820 – b. bet. 1776-1794; 1830 census – b. bet. 1781-1790.

theorize that John is Henry Kidd's eldest son and has inherited Henry's land. In 1821, his LTL entry is listed as John Kidd Jr., to distinguish him from John Kidd Sr. Beginning in 1833, his estate is listed for three years until 1835:

Year	NAME	Acres	Description	CH	COMMENTS
1804	John Kidd	81½			
1805-1813	John Kidd	81¾			
1814-1815	John Kidd	81¾	Adj Wm Campbell	9SE	
1816-1820	John Kidd	81¾	Adj Wm Campbell Estate	9SE	
1821-1826	John Kidd **Jr.**	81¾	Adj Wm Campbell Estate	9SE	
1827-1832	John Kidd Jr.	81¾	Adj Jacob Hart	9SE	
1833-1835	John Kidd Jr. **Est.**	81¾	Adj Jacob Hart	9SE	

In 1836, his estate drops from the annual LTLs, and that same year adjoining neighbor Jacob Hart's land holdings have increased by 160 acres, at least some of it noted as being "of Kidd's estate."

1810 – A **John Kidd** is on the federal census for K&Q Co, p. 168/221 (mis-indexed as RIDD on Ancestry.com), line 3 from bottom:
Kidd, John B [?]. 20100-00100 (2M<10 & 1 16-25; 1F 16-25) and three slaves.
[The B does not appear to be an initial, but instead a symbol of some sort, as it's quite flourished and not like other capital Bs on the census page.]

1810-1820 – TWO John Kidds continue to appear annually on the K&Q PPTLs in these years, distinguished both by residing in different districts and by their relative wealth.
This John Kidd lived in the southern district of K&Q (in Stratton Major Parish) and owned less land and fewer slaves than the other John Kidd. This John Kidd is listed in bold, below.

YEAR	TAXPAYER	WT	B>16	B 12 -16	H	Cows	COMMENTS
1810	**John Kidd**	1	1	0	2		Faulkner's list
1810	John Kidd	1	8	2	5		Hoskins' List; 2 gigs & Merchant's license
1811	**John Kidd**	1	0	0	2		Faulkner's list
1811	John Kidd	2	7	1	5		Hoskins' List; 2-wh carriage
1812	**John Kidd**	1	0	1	1		Faulkner's list

1812	John Kidd	2	7	1	5		Hoskins' List; 2-wh carriage
1813	**John Kidd**	1	0	1	1		Faulkner's List
1813	John Kidd	2	8	2	5		Hoskins' list; 1 2-wh carriage $80
1814	**John Kidd**	1	0	2	1		Fleet's list
1814	John Kidd	2	8	1	5		Hoskin's list
1815	John Kidd	2	8	3	5		Courtney's L
1815	**John Kidd**	1	2	0	2	8	Francis Row's L
1816	John Kidd	3	8	2	6		Courtney's L
1816	**John Kidd**	1	1	0	1		Francis Row's L
1817	**John Kidd**	1	1	0	1		Francis Row's L
1818	John Kidd	3	7	2	6		Courtney's L
1818	**John Kidd**	1	2	0	2		Francis Row's L
1819	John Kidd	2	9	1	5		Courtney's L
1819	**John Kidd**	1	3	0	2		Francis Row's L
1820	John Kidd	1	9	4	4		Courtney's L
1820	**John Kidd**	1	3	0	2		Francis Row's L

1820 – There are two **John Kidds** on the federal census for K&Q Co, but the John Kidd of Stratton Major Parish, the southern parish, is consistent with the 1810 census and PPTLs and LTLs for this John Kidd:
Page 55, Stratton Major Parish
John Kidd – 2M<10 & 1 26-44; 3F<10 and one 16-25, plus 8 slaves. Total=15, with 5 in agriculture.

1821-1827 – In these years, there continue to be TWO John Kidds on the PPTLs of K&Q County, as depicted by the Tables below. From 1821 onward, K&Q had one consolidated PPTL list per year (rather than two tax districts with separate lists in the earlier years.

YEAR	DATE	TAXPAYER	B>12	H	COMMENTS
1821	7-Apr	John Kidd	13	6	2 gigs ($30 ea)
1821	10-Apr	**John Kidd Jr.**	1	2	1 gig ($20)
1822	6-Apr	John Kidd	11	7	1 gig ($40)
1822	25-Mar	**John Kidd Jr.**	0	2	1 gig ($20)

YEAR	DATE	TAXPAYER	WMT	B>16	B 12-16	H	COMMENTS
1823	25-Apr	Jno. D.? Kidd	1	9	3	7	2 gigs ($40 each)
1823	7-Mar	**John Kidd**	1	1	0	2	1 gig ($20)
1824	5-Mar	**John Kidd**	1	1	0	2	1 gig ($20)
1824	30-Apr	John Kidd	1	11	1	6	1 gig ($30)
1825	14-Mar	**John Kidd**	1	1	0	2	1 gig ($20)
1825	30-Apr	John Kidd	1	11	1	6	1 gig ($25)
1826	4-May	John Kidd	1	11	1	5	2 gigs ($50)
1826	18-May	**John ("below")**	1	1	0	2	1 gig ($20)

1823 – 07 Sept. 1823. Johanna Baker, William Baker & wife Maria, Mary Baker, Sarah Pace of Middlesex, **John Kidd & wife Jane of King & Queen County** to Thomas Groom of Middlesex. For $100. 82 acres of "land whereon George Dunton died possessed of." No further description. Witnessed by Samuel May (for John and Jane Kidd), Jos. M. Lipscomb (for Johanna Baker and William Baker), and [Robt?] Healey & Zack W. Bristow (for Mary Baker and Sarah Pace).[98]

1829 – A land survey was performed in the name of "**John Kidd Jr.,** from Robert M. Spencer."[99] This survey shows a tract of 365 acres in K&Q County and Stratton Major Parish, and, despite the title, this **John Kidd** was not the grantee, but one of the bounding neighbors.

1830 – 25 June 1830. William Baker & wife Maria of Middlesex County, and Sarah Pace, **John Kidd & wife Jane,** John Garnett & wife Polly [this is likely Mary Baker in the 1823 deed above] all of King & Queen Co. To Thomas Healey of Middlesex Co. For $60. 52 acres of land "being part of the [xxx] School tract of land." Not witnessed. **John Kidd** signed by mark "x." Jane Kidd did not sign but relinquished her dower on 25 June 1830.[100]

1830 – there are three **John Kidds** on the federal census in K&Q Co; the last entry matches this John Kidd, now identified as John Kidd Sr.:

page 274, line 11:

John Kidd – 2M 30-39, 1 60-69;1F 15-19, 1 20-29 & 1 60-69, and 24 slaves.

page 296, line 13:
John Kidd Jr. – 1M & 1F, both 20-29, and no slaves.

---

[98] MSX DB 15, pp. 12-13 (in Craig Kilby's "Kidd MSX Deed Books 12-22" document, now in the MSX Shared Folder.)
[99] King and Queen County Land Plat Book, 1822-1881, LoV reel 21, reviewed by RK in July 2018, page 43.
   John Kidd's name appears only as a neighbor on the actual land plat, but the Index entry reads "Kidd, John jr. from Spencer Robert M, p 43." Images of both the plat and the index entry available upon request.
[100] MSEX DB 16, p. 479-481. CK writes, " I did not scan page 481 which included the date of recording."

page 296, line 15:
John Kidd Sr. – 3M<5 & 1 40-49; 1F 5-9, 1 10-14, & 1 15-19, and 4 slaves.

1833 – the **John Kidd Jr. Estate** appears on the 1833 LTLs; he has died in the past twelve months. See LTLs above; his estate appears though 1835, when the land apparently is acquired by neighbor Jacob Hart.

1835 – 23 Feb 1835. William Baker of MSX Co named guardian to William Kidd and Robert Kidd, orphans of **John Kidd**. William Baker and William Shepherd security for $400 bond."[101] [William Baker, guardian to John Kidd's orphans, is likely his brother-in-law and co-grantor with John Kidd on the 1823 and 1830 deeds above.]

<u>JOHN KIDD (3)</u>, the son of William Kidd Sr. of Caroline County
John5 (William4, Daniel3, Thomas2, Thomas1) Kidd].
 Also known as John Kidd of Lumpkin and Co. and also as John Kidd Sr.
Born in 1769 in Caroline Co.
Left records in Caroline Co. until 1808, when he's first found in K&Q records.
His land was 30 miles northwest of K&Q Courthouse on the Mattapony River in Drysdale or St. Stephen's Parish, close to the Caroline county line.[102]
Married Ann [last name likely was Lumpkin].
Died in K&Q Co on 23 May 1839.

This John Kidd was very wealthy, more so than the other John Kidds in K&Q Co.
He first appears in K&Q Co in 1808, which coincides with the disappearance of John Kidd from Caroline Co.

The children of John Kidd(3) and his wife Ann (likely a Lumpkin) were:
 1. John (M.?) Kidd John Kidd(4) - likely born about 1803; married Catherine F. Boulware; died in 1836 (before his father's death) and his children were named in the will of John Kidd(3). See his section below.
 2. Maria Kidd -- birth and death dates unknown; married James W. Upshaw in K&Q County. Predeceased her father, and her children are also named in the will of John Kidd(3).
 3. Ann Kidd -- born about 1790; never married. She died in 1838, a year before her father, and she's therefore not named in his will. But her will names two of her sisters, Elizabeth Kidd and Mary Ann (Kidd) Bagby, as her heirs.
 4. Elizabeth Kidd – born abt 1799; married first Edwin Motley, who died by 1837, and second married John Bagby (1791-1880). Neither she nor her children are named in her father's will.
 5. Mary Ann Kidd – born in 1809 in King and Queen Co. Married Travis Bagby; named in her father's will. Died in 1874.

---

[101] MSX Guardian Bonds, 1832-1836, p. 160
[102] According to Alfred Bagby's 1908 book on King and Queen county, "**John Kidd Sr.** lived near Munday's Bridge. Munday's Bridge was in the northwest part of K&Q County, southwest of the community of Newtown. It crossed the Mattapony River, which is the border between K&Q County to the NE and King Willliam County to the SW. Just a few miles north of Munday's bridge is the boundary between K&Q to the east, and the southeastern tip of Caroline County on the west.

6. Tom [Thomas], named as a son of John Kidd in an 1821 Sheriff's Account Book for K&Q Co, and John Kidd .

Not dated -- In *King and Queen County, Virginia* by Rev. Alfred Bagby, 1908, p.366, in a section titled "Fragments", Bagby names "Kidd. – **John Kidd Sr.,** lived near Munday's Bridge. Children: John, Mary (Bagby), Elizabeth (Motley and Bagby), John Jr., the father of John B. Kidd."[103] [Note: Bagby names son John twice, but does not mention John Sr.'s daughter Maria or son Thomas. This appears to be from his knowledge of local families.]

1790-1791 – an adult **John Kidd** appears for the first time on the **Caroline Co PPTLs** in 1790, in the district of Nicholas Long; he's taxed for his own tithe, and one horse. This is consistent with his birth year of 1769. His listing is unchanged in 1791. He then drops from these PPTLs until 1796 (see below)

1796 – a **John Kidd** again appears on the **Caroline Co PPTL** in 1796, on the list of William Jones, taxed for his own tithe, one slave over 16, and one horse. I don't find him there in 1797, but the images are very faded, and he could be overlooked on this PPTL.

1798-1807 – a **John Kidd** appears on the **Caroline Co PPTLs** in each of these years, each year taxed for only one white male tithe and with slaves starting in 1796.

Year	Taxpayer	WMT	B> 16	B 12 -16	H	COMMENTS
1790	John Kidd	1	0	0	1	
1791	John Kidd	1	0	0	1	
1792-1795	Not listed in Caroline					
1796	John Kidd	1	1	1	1	
1797	Not listed in Caroline					
1798	John Kidd	1	1	1	3	
1799	John Kidd	1	2	1	1	
1800	John Kidd	1	2	0	4	
1801	John Kidd	1	2	0	4	
1802	John Kidd	1	2	0	4	
1803	John Kidd	1	2	1	4	
1804	John Kidd	1	2	1	4	
1805	John Kidd	1	2	1	3	
1806	John Kidd	1	2	1	2	

---

[103] *King and Queen County, Virginia*, by Rev. Alfred **Bagby**, Regional Publishing Co., Baltimore, MD, 1973. (The original book was published in 1908.) This book is available online in the catalog at Familysearch.org and Ancestry.com.

Year	Taxpayer	WMT	B> 16	B 12 -16	H	COMMENTS
1807	John Kidd	1	2	1	3	

[There was no tax statewide in 1808. In 1809, a different John Kidd, with no slaves, appears in Caroline with the notation "grandson to Wm."]

1800 – Caroline County Court records for October 1800, listing the payments to various citizens for Patrole services, include a payment of $1.32 to **John Kidd**.

1802 - Caroline County Court records for October 1802, listing the payments to various citizens for Patrole services, includes a payment to **John Kidd** ($1.44).[104]

1803 – In Caroline Co February Court 1803, the division of the estate of William Kidd was recorded, naming his widow, Mary, and their surviving children: James, Philip, Henry, Thomas, Willis, Edmund, **John**, Fanny (the wife of Washington Jones), Walker, Joel, Polly, and Elizabeth (wife of Edwin Motley).[105], [106]

1804 – In Caroline Co December 1804, a Chancery suit was heard involving the estate of Thomas Kidd, dec'd [the son of William Kidd Sr.]. This suit names Thomas's three heirs as his widow, Elizabeth; his daughter, Lucy, who was the wife of Mattthew Hundley; and a minor son named William. One account of this record names the guardian of this minor as **John Kidd**.[107]

1805-1812 – a **John Kidd** appears on the Caroline Co LTLs for the first time in 1805, after he has received 26 acres from his father William Kidd's estate.[108] This listing recurs annually through 1812. The Land Alterations schedule of the 1812 LTL shows that **John Kidd** and his brother Walker Kidd each transferred their 26 acres to their sister Fanny Kidd Jones.

1808 – On 5 October 1808 **John Kidd** and Walker Kidd were witnesses to the will of Edwin Motley in K&Q Co Virginia.[109] John and Walker's sister Elizabeth Kidd married Edwin Motley.

1809 – A third **John Kidd** appears on the annual K&Q LTLs (there was no tax statewide in 1808). This John Kidd is listed as "**John Kidd of Lumpkin & Co.**" and is taxed on 214 acres. This entry recurs annually until 1813, when the K&Q LTL for this year lists him only as "John Kidd" (dropping the "of Lumpkin and Co." notation), but the land parcel is unchanged, at 214 acres.

---

[104] *Caroline County, Virginia Court Records: probate and other records from the Court Order and Minute Books, 1800-1804, Vol. 3*, by Kimberly Curtis Campbell, Athens, GA 2001, p. 93.

[105] *Caroline County, Virginia Court Records: probate and other records from the Court Order and Minute Books, 1800-1804, Vol. 3*, by Kimberly Curtis Campbell, Athens, GA 2001, pp. 23-24

[106] Caroline County Order Book, 1802-1804, page 130-134, retrieved from FHL #1887726 (restricted access, FHCs only), images 336-338. Digital images available upon request.

[107] *Caroline County, Virginia Court Records: probate and other records from the Court Order and Minute Books, 1800-1804, Vol. 3*, by Kimberly Curtis Campbell, Athens, GA 2001, p. 41.

[108] This seems to prove that the John Kidd on these LTLs was indeed William Kidd Sr.'s son, and not his grandson.

[109] This will and codicils are online at the Library of Virginia web site at virginiamemory.com/collections/lost. Once there, search on Motley. A digital copy of this will is available from the authors, or via this website.

The K&Q LTLs for 1814 & 1815 each have two entries for this **John Kidd**; he's taxed on 178 acres owned "in fee" and bearing the notation, "Mattapony & Eubanks orphans," and he's taxed also on 105 acres, "part in fee and part in dower" and bearing the notations, "of Lumpkin's Estate" and "Betsy Lumpkin, adj. above land". In 1816, the acreage drops slightly by 6 acres, with no notation as to what become of the 6 acres. In 1818, the two parcels are combined and the notation "part for life" appears on the LTLs. This notes that the part of the Lumpkin land, noted as in dower, was inherited through John's wife, which means that she may have been a Lumpkin before her marriage.

In 1822, **John Kidd's** LTL entries add 30 acres from Andrew B. Motley.

In 1823, **John Kidd's** LTL entries add 47 acres from Thomas Kidd, who is noted as his son when John pays tax on "47 acres belonging to son Tom" in an 1821 Sheriff's Account Book for K&Q Co.

See the Table below for John's LTL entries. The **John Kidd Estate** appears in 1839 and 1840, and disappears in 1841.

Year	NAME	Acres	Description	CH	COMMENTS
1809-1813	John Kidd of Lumpkin & Co.	214			
1814-1815	John Kidd	178 105	Adj Mattapony & Eubank orphans - Betsy Lumpkin	30NW	- "of Lumpkin Estate" "Part in fee and part in dower"
1816-1817	John Kidd	172 105	Adj Mattapony R orphans & Betsy Lumpkin	30NW	
1818-1819	John Kidd	277	adj The Mattapony R. & Betsy Lumpkin	30NW	"part for Life"; John inherited part of the 105 acre tract through his wife
1820-1821	John Kidd	277	The Mattapony R.	30NW	
1822	John Kidd	277 30	The Mattapony R.	30NW 30NW	- "of Andrew B. Motley"
1823-1828	John Kidd	277 30 47	The Mattapony R. adj. the above adj. the above	30NW	- "of Andrew B. Motley" "of Thomas Kidd"
1829-1833	John Kidd **Sr.**	374	Mattapony R. & Thos Dunn	30NW	
1834-1835	John Kidd	374 72	(as above) adjoining the above	30NW	- "of Hawes (Hanes?) Est."

Year	NAME	Acres	Description	CH	COMMENTS
1836-1838	John Kidd	446	As above	30NW	(acreage combined in 1836)
1839-1840	John Kidd Est.	446	As above	30NW	In 1840, adj "Mrs Mann & children"

1809 – This **John Kidd** is listed in the K&Q Co PPTLs for 1809 through 1839. Entries for this John Kidd begin to appear as "John Kidd Sr." in 1827, and continue most years through 1837. The 1840 PPTL lists the **John Kidd Estate**. From the tax lists, it is clear that this John Kidd was very wealthy:

Year	Taxpayer	WMT	B> 16	B 12 -16	H	COMMENTS
1809	Kidd, John	1	6	0	4	2 (riding)chairs
1810	Kidd, John	1	8	2	5	2 gigs
1811	Kidd, John	2	7	1	5	2-wh carriage
1812	Kidd, John	2	7	1	5	1 2-wh carriage
1813	Kidd, John	2	8	2	5	1 2-wh carriage ($80)
1814	Kidd, John	2	8	1	5	1 gig
1815	Kidd, John	2	8	2	5	1 slave 9-12; gig ($45)
1816	Kidd, John	3	8	2	6	1 gig ($45)
1817	Kidd, John	4	8	3	5	1 gig ($25)
1818	Kidd, John	3	7	2	6	
1819	Kidd, John	2	9	1	5	2 gigs, $60 each
1820	Kidd, John	1	9	4	4	2 gigs ($60 each)
1821	Kidd, John	-	-	-	6	11 slaves >12; 2 gigs ($30 each)
1822	Kidd, John	-	-	-	7	11 slaves>12; 1 gig ($40)
1823	Kidd, Jno. D. ?	1	9	3	7	2 gigs ($40 each)
1824	Kidd, John	1	11	1	6	1 gig ($30)
1825	Kidd, John	1	11	1	6	1 gig ($25)
1826	Kidd, John	1	11	1	5	2 gigs ($50)
1827	Kidd, John Sr.	-	-	-	6	15 B>12; 1 gig ($50)
1828	Kidd, John Sr.	-	-	-	6	13 B>12; 2 gigs ($50 each)
1829	Kidd, John Sr.	-	-	-	7	9 B>12; 2 gigs ($25 each)

Year	Taxpayer	WMT	B> 16	B 12 -16	H	COMMENTS
1830	Kidd, John Sr.	-	-	-	7	11 B>12; 2 gigs ($40 each)
1831	Kidd, John Sr.	-	-	-	4	12 B>12
1832	Kidd, John	-	-	-	4	12 B>12
1833	Kidd, John Sr.	-	-	-	6	11 B>12; 2 gigs ($25 each)
1834	Kidd, John Sr.	-	-	-	6	13 b>12; 1 gig ($75)
1835	Kidd, John "u. C."	-	-	-	5	12 B>12; 2 gigs ($100 & $60)
1836	Kidd, John Sr.	-	-	-	4	10 B>12; 2 gigs ($90 & $60)
1837	Kidd, John Sr.	-	-	-	4	10 B>12; 2 gigs ($90 & $60)
1838	Kidd, John	-	-	-	4	12 B>12
1839	Kidd, John	-	-	-	4	11 B>12; 1 gig ($60)
1840	Kidd, John ESTATE	-	-	-	3	10 B>12

[Note: In 1821 and 1822 (and again, in 1827, ff.), the K&Q Co PPTLs did not list WMTs and had one column for slaves.]

[Note: Joel H. Kidd and Richard Kidd first appear on the K&Q Co PPTLs in 1841, each with slaves, but it is not known if they would have inherited from John Kidd. Joel H. Kidd was John's nephew and the son of Willis Kidd of Caroline Co. We do not know the identity of this Richard Kidd.]

1810 – One **John Kidd** is on the federal census in K&Q Co this year, with a large household and a number of slaves consistent with the PPTLs for this John Kidd:
p. 222B, line 3:

John Kidd Sr. – 4M<10, 1 16-25 & 2 26-44; 3F<10, 2 10-15 & 2 26-44, and 22 slaves.

1820 – There are two **John Kidds** on the federal census for K&Q Co, but the John Kidd of Drysdale Parish[110] is consistent with the 1810 census and PPTLs for this John:
Page 55, Drysdale (the northern) Parish:
John Kidd – 1M<10, 1 16-18, 4 16-25, 1 26-44 & 1 45 and up; 1F 10-15, 2 16-25 and 1 45 and up, and 23 slaves. Total 35, with 8 in agriculture & 4 in manufacturing and trades.

1821 – **John Kidd** pays taxes on his **son Tom's** account, as recorded in a King & Queen County Sheriff's Account Book, 1821:

John Kidd
Tax on 277 Acres Land   3.00
    47 do belonging to **son Tom**   .51
    13 negroes   6.89

---

[110] According to http://vagenweb.org/parishes.htm by Freddie Spradlin, Drysdale Parish was formed in 1723 from St. Stephen's Parish in King & Queen County. When Caroline County was formed in 1728 from parts of Essex, King & Queen and King William Counties, Drysdale Parish served parts of both Caroline and K&Q counties.

6 horses 81¢. 2 gigs $1	1.81
10 County and poor rates	6.30
~~m fine~~	~~.75~~
	$18.51
To amt brt up	19.26
1820	
tax on 1 County and poor rates	
for **William Kidd**	1.05
By Poor Order	8.00
	18.51
By Cash	10.51
	$18.51[111]

1826 - Married on 15 Ult.[Jan] by Rev. Thomas M. Henley, Dr. James W. Upshaw of Caroline Co., to Miss Maria Kidd, daughter of Mr. **John Kidd** of King & Queen Co.[112]   Maria evidently had died by 1839, when her father's will left bequests to her three children James M. D. Upshaw, Thomas E. Upshaw and Sarah Ann Upshaw.[113]

1828-1832 – the first appearance of this **John Kidd** "of K&Q" occurs on the **Caroline Co** VA 1828 LTL, when he appears with 354¼ acres, with no indication of when and where he acquired this land, which, **listed as John Kidd Sr.**, he then transfers to his son **John Kidd Jr.** in 1830.

Year	NAME	Acres	Description	CH	COMMENTS
1828-1829	John Kidd	354¼	R.L. Blackburn	12E	"Of K&Q"; Daniel Turner's district
1830	**John Kidd Sr.** John Kidd Jr.	- 354¼	R.L. Blackburn	12E	"transferred to John Kidd Jr." **"from John Kidd Senr."**
1831	John Kidd Jr.	354¼	R.L. Blackburn	12E	"of K&Q Co."
1832	John Kidd Jr.	-	-	-	354¼ acres to Robert Andrews
1833	Drops from	These	LTLs		

1830 – There are **three John Kidds** on the 1830 federal census in K&Q Co. This John Kidd is the first one listed, with the largest holding of slaves:
page 274, line 11:
John Kidd – 2M 30-39, 1 60-69;1F 15-19, 1 20-29 & 1 60-69, and 24 slaves
page 296, line 13:

---

[111] In the article, "King and Queen Sheriff's Account Book, 1821 (continued)," by Susan B. Chiarello, *Magazine of Virginia Genealogy*, volume 51, page 255. Scanned images in the K&Q Source Documents folder.

[112] *Marriages and Deaths from Richmond, Virginia Newspapers 1780-1820*. Special Publication No. 8. Richmond, VA: Virginia Historical Society, 1983, p. 181, citing the *Richmond Enquirer*, 19 Jan 1826, p. 3 (from Craig Kilby).

[113] The original will was lost with the other K&Q records. Fortunately, a certified copy was made at some point, and was passed down in the family of John Boulware Kidd, this John Kidd's grandson. It is now part of the Ellen Gertrude Tompkins Kidd papers, 1791-1998, Accession 52005. Personal papers collection, The Library of Virginia, Richmond, VA. Photographed and transcribed by RK there, July 2018.

John Kidd Jr. – 1M & 1F, both 20-29, and no slaves
page 296, line 15:
John Kidd Sr. – 3M<5 & 1 40-49; 1F 5-9, 1 10-14, & 1 15-19, and 4 slaves

1835 – 12 June 1835. **John Kidd** and Travis Bagby, appellants, against James M. Jeffries, appellee}
On an appeal from the decision of County Court of King and Queen on 9 February 1835
granting letters of administration of all the goods, chattels and credits of Thos. J. Grisham,
deceased, to the appellee…the Court heard the arguments, as well as testimony from
multiple witnesses, and decided that there had been no error in judgment. They ruled that
the appellants pay the court costs of the appellee.[114]

1839 – **John Kidd** signed his will on 15 May 1839 in K&Q Co. This lengthy compilation names as
his heirs his wife Ann; his daughter Mary Ann Bagby, wife of Travis Bagby; his three
grandchildren, James M. D. Upshaw, Thomas E. Upshaw and Sarah Ann Upshaw, the
children of his daughter Maria Upshaw, apparently deceased; and his two grandchildren
Maria D. Kidd and John B. Kidd, the children of his deceased son John Kidd (who died in
1836). His will does not name his daughter Elizabeth Motley or her children, nor his son
Tom [Thomas]. He appointed his son-in-law Travis Bagby and his friend James Smith as his
executors.

This will was proven in K&Q Co Court on 8 July 1839.[115]

John Kidd died 23 May 1839, according to the Bagby family Bible[116]; this date of death is
also confirmed in the *Religious Herald* issue of 28 June 1839. His estate appears on the 1840
K&Q PPTL and on the 1840 federal census (see below).

The Bagby family Bible contains these entries:
"**John Kidd** father of Mary Ann Bagby wife of Travis Bagby died 23 May 1839 aged 70"
"Ann Kidd, wife of **John Kidd**, and mother of Mary Ann Bagby died April 14th, 1847 aged
80 years.

The *Religious Herald* entries read:
"Issue of 28 June 1839. Died, at his residence in King and Queen County, on the 23rd day of
May Mr. **John Kidd** in the 70th year of his age."
"Issue of 22 July 1847. The widow of brother **John Kidd**...died April 14 of the current year
at the residence of her son-in-law Travis Bagby, aged 80 years."

1840 – The **John Kidd Estate** appears on the Caroline Co VA PPTL for this year, taxed on only 1
horse and a gig valued at $45. This is likely the estate of John Kidd Sr., who died in K&Q

---

[114] *K&Q Superior Court of Law & Chancery Records, 1831-1851*, p. 58, retrieved from FHL #32114, image 88. Scanned
image of this document is available in the K&Q Source Documents folder and the K&Q Court records subfolder.

[115] The original will was lost with the other K&Q records. Fortunately, a certified copy was made at some point, and
was passed down in the family of John Boulware Kidd, this John Kidd's grandson. It is now part of the Ellen
Gertrude Tompkins Kidd papers, 1791-1998, Accession 52005. Personal papers collection, The Library of Virginia,
Richmond, VA. Photographed and transcribed by RK there, July 2018.

[116] Bagby Family Bible (1750-1860), Virginia Historical Society Acc. Mss6:4 B1465:1. A transcription of this bible is
found in *Bible Records of Caroline County, Virginia Families*, by Herbert Ridgeway Collins, Heritage Books, Westminster,
MD, 2008, pp. 10-ff. A card index for this (and many other Virginia family Bibles) is available at
www.familysearch.org/search/collection/1932510

Co, but who also had property in Caroline County as demonstrated in the above Caroline LTLs. The estate then drops from these tax lists.

1840 – The **John Kidd Estate** also is found on the 1840 federal census in K&Q Co, page 86, line 5, under the name of his son-in-law and executor Travis Bagby. This is an unusual notation, but the full entry on the census reads "Travis Bagby Exr. **Jno. Kidd**." This household includes 2M 10-15 and 1 20-29; and 1F 40-49, along with 23 slaves, with 10 engaged in agriculture. It is unclear whether the white household represents John's family or the family of Travis Bagby, but the estate is clearly that of the wealthy John Kidd.

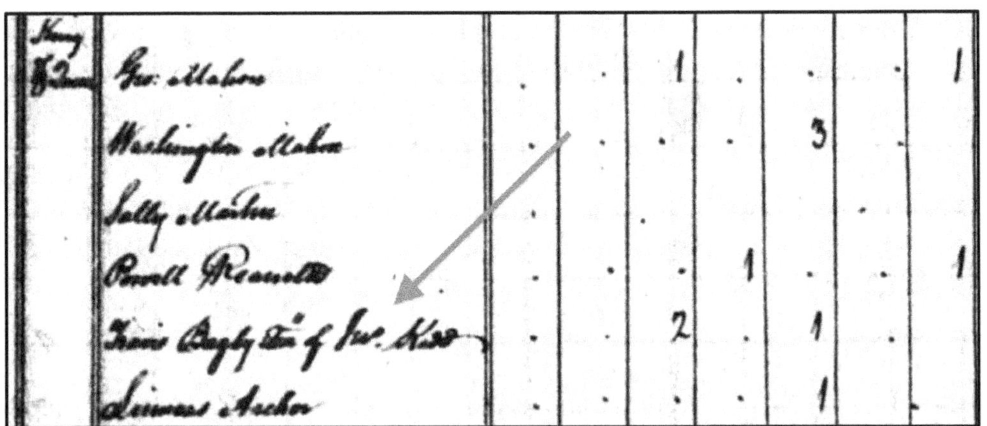

FIGURE: A screenshot of the entry for John Kidd's estate on the 1840 federal census for King & Queen County, Virginia, listed here under the name of his executor, Travis Bagby.

Travis Bagby, executor of **John Kidd, deceased**, ran this advertisement in the Richmond Enquirer on Aug 21, 1840,[117] advertising 446 acres of land owned by John Kidd, deceased, lying 3 miles from New Town and 8 from Ayletts:

MATTAPONY LAND FOR SALE.—As Executor of John Kidd, deceased, and pursuant to a decree of the County Court of King and Queen, pronounced the 13th day of July, 1840, I shall proceed to sell, to the highest bidder, on the premises, on the 10th day of September next, if fair, if not, the next fair day, on a credit of twelve months, that valuable estate whereon the said John Kidd died seized and possessed, lying in the county of King & Queen, about three miles from New Town and eight from Ayletts, containing four hundred and forty-six acres. The land is fertile, very level, and easy to cultivate. The improvements are a good dwelling-house, with eight rooms, and the necessary out-houses.

The manager, living on the premises, or myself, about three miles distant, will take pleasure in showing the land to any person wishing to view it.   TRAVIS BAGBY.
August 7   26—w4w

1842 – 4 May 1842. Travis Bagby, executor of **John Kidd, deceased**, plaintiff against Charles James Fox, James B. Harrison and Edward S. Acree, defendants}A motion for a judgment and an

---

[117] America's Genealogybank.com

award from execution on a bond entered into by the defendants for the forthcoming and delivery of certain property taken to satisfy the plaintiffs' execution…

The court ruled in favor of the plaintiff, and decreed that he recover from the defendants $209.88, the penalty of the said bond, and his costs. The defendants plead in mercy, and the judgment was cut in half, with interest from 16 January 1842 till paid, plus plaintiff's costs.[118]

JOHN KIDD (4), the son of John Kidd(3) of K&Q County

John6 (John5, William4, Daniel3, Thomas2, Thomas1) Kidd
Date of birth unknown but probably about 1803,[119] likely in Caroline Co. Records found in both K&Q and Caroline Cos.
Married Catherine F. Boulware.
Children were Maria Kidd and John B. Kidd.
Died 26 September 1836 in K&Q County.

His middle initial was M., according to his son John B. Kidd's obituary. We have found no original records that include a middle initial or middle name for this John Kidd during his lifetime. A photograph of what is purported to be his headstone[120] shows the inscription: In memory of JOHN KIDD, Born July 30th, 1800, Died Sept. 26, 1836." It seems likely that the middle initial, M, may have been added by later generations.

Not dated -- In *King and Queen County, Virginia* by Rev. Alfred Bagby, 1908, p.366, in a section titled "Fragments", Bagby names "Kidd. – John Kidd Sr., lived near Munday's Bridge. Children: John, Mary (Bagby), Elizabeth (Motley and Bagby), **John Jr.**, the father of John B. Kidd."[121]

1810 – This **John Kidd** is likely one of the white males under the age of ten in his father John Kidd Sr.'s household on the federal census for K&Q Co:

p. 222B, line 3: John Kidd Sr. – **4M<10,** 1 16-25 & 2 26-44; 3F<10, 2 10-15 & 2 26-44, and 22 slaves.

1820 – There are two John Kidds on the federal census for K&Q this year. This **John Kidd** is likely in the household of his father John Kidd(3) of Drysdale Parish[122]:
Page 55, Drysdale (the northern) parish:

---

[118] *K&Q Superior Court of Law & Chancery Records, 1831-1851*, pp. 237-238, retrieved from FHL #32114, images 265-266. Scanned images of this document are available in the K&Q Source Documents folder and the K&Q Court records subfolder.

[119] This estimated year of birth comes from what we believe are his census entries for 1830 (age 20-29), 1820 (age 16-18) and 1810 (under 10). If we're right about his position on the 1820 census (in conjunction with the other two censuses) he was born between 1802-1804. HOWEVER, his headstone states that he was born 30 July 1800, and that he died 26 Sept. 1836.

[120] This image is attached to several family trees, but no details are provided as to the location of the cemetery where he is buried. Nevertheless, the date of death corresponds with this John Kidd's obituary, and thus it is plausible.

[121] *King and Queen County, Virginia*, by Rev. Alfred **Bagby**, Regional Publishing Co., Baltimore, MD, 1973. (The original book was published in 1908.) This book is available online in the catalog at Familysearch.org and Ancestry.com.

[122] According to http://vagenweb.org/parishes.htm by Freddie Spradlin, Drysdale Parish was formed in 1723 from St. Stephen's Parish in King & Queen County. When Caroline County was formed in 1728 from parts of Essex, King & Queen and King William Counties, Drysdale Parish served parts of both Caroline and K&Q counties.

John Kidd – 1M<10, 1 16-18, 4 16-25, 1 26-44 & 1 45 and up; 1F 10-15, 2 16-25 and 1 45 and up, and 23 slaves. Total =35, with 8 in agriculture & 4 in manufacturing and trades.

1825 – On 27 May 1825, a **John Kidd** was a chain carrier for a survey of land in K&Q Co for John Collins and Edward Garrett, who were having a land dispute.[123]

1830-1832 – **John Kidd Jr. "of K&Q Co"** appears on the Caroline Co LTL in 1830 when his father John Kidd Sr. transfers to him a tract of 354¼ acres. This entry drops from the LTLs in 1833.

Year	NAME	Acres	Description	CH	COMMENTS
1828-1829	John Kidd	354¼	R.L. Blackburn	12E	"Of K&Q"; Daniel Turner's district
1830	John Kidd Sr. **John Kidd Jr.**	354¼	R.L. Blackburn	12E	"transferred to John Kidd Jr." "from John Kidd Senr."
1831	John Kidd Jr.	354¼	R.L. Blackburn	12E	"of K&Q Co."
1832	John Kidd Jr.	-	-	-	354¼ acres to Robert Andrews
1833	Drops from	These	LTLs		

1830 – there are **three John Kidds** on the federal census in K&Q Co. in this year. This John Kidd is likely the one listed as **John Kidd, Jr** (second entry below):
page 274, line 11:
John Kidd – 2M 30-39, 1 60-69;1F 15-19, 1 20-29 & 1 60-69, and 24 slaves.
page 296, line 13:
John Kidd Jr. – 1M & 1F, both 20-29, and no slaves.
page 296, line 15:
John Kidd Sr. – 3M<5 & 1 40-49; 1F 5-9, 1 10-14, & 1 15-19, plus 4 slaves.

1833 – a **John Kidd, Jr.** appears on the annual Caroline Co VA PPTLs in 1833, 1834, 1836, and 1837, taxed only for his own tithe. Since he died in K&Q Co, and was no longer taxed for land in Caroline Co, it is not known why he is on the Caroline PPTLs:

Year	Taxpayer	WMT	B> 16	B 12 -16	H	COMMENTS
1833	John Kidd Jr.	1	0	0	0	
1834	John Kidd Jr.	1	0	0	0	
1835	Not found					
1836	John Kidd Jr.	1	0	0	0	
1837	John Kidd Jr.	1	0	0	0	

---

[123] King and Queen County Land Plat Book, 1822-1881, LoV reel 21, reviewed by RK in July 2018. I just happened to notice his name in this record as I was searching for other records. Scanned image available upon request.

Year	Taxpayer	WMT	B> 16	B 12 -16	H	COMMENTS
1838	Not found					

1836 – On Friday, 7 Oct 1836, **John Kidd Jr.'s** obituary appeared in the *Richmond Enquirer*, p. 3, noting his death at New Town in K&Q Co on 26 September 1836. The obituary mentions (though not by name) that his wife, two infant children, and parents mourn him, indicating they are still living at the time of his death.

DEATH

Died, at New Town, King and Queen county, on the 26th ult. John Kidd, jr. The deceased had scarcely reached the meridian of life when death selected him as a victim, and now all that remains of his mortal part is laid low in the silent grave. In his usual health, and with every reason to look forward to many years of enjoyment, he was suddenly taken off, by a rapid fever of only a few days' duration. He seemed, from the commencement, to have a presentiment of the final result; yet he complained not, neither of the ague's long and icy chill, nor of the fever's scorching heat, nor of his anticipated fate. He has left many to bewail the bereavement they have sustained in the loss of one, who, as a friend, was sincere and devoted; as a neighbor, was kind and attentive; as a gentleman, was polished, literary and intelligent; and who acted well his part in all the various relations of life. The poor lament in his decease the loss of a benefactor. But a wife and two infant children have suffered a loss that no time nor circumstance can repair. Upon them he had concentrated the warm affection of his heart, and there glowed with intensity all the tenderness of his ardent nature. In the relation of a son, he was also conspicuous for the attention and regard which he always manifested. His parents reposed on him as a staff for their support in their declining years, as one who would soothe and alleviate the afflictions that attend the descent of old age to the tomb. But, alas! their staff is broken, their fond hopes are blasted; the source of their pleasures, their consolations and their anticipations, is torn from them. The world, I doubt not, has lost much of its charm, and looks dark, dreary and desolate. May the father of the fatherless, and the husband of the widow, comfort also the afflicted parents.

1837-1839 – the **John Kidd Junr Estate** appears on the K&Q LTLs for 1837-1839 and drops from the list in 1840. The location of this land, in the northwest part of the county, is close to the land of his father John Kidd Sr.

Year	NAME	Acres	Description	CH	COMMENTS
1837	John Kidd Junr Estate	275		22 NW	Adjoining "Mrs. Mann and children"
1838	John Kidd Junr Estate	- 275		22 NW	Adjoining Mrs. Mann and children
1839	John Kidd Junr Estate	275		22 NW	Adjoining Mrs. Mann and children

Year	NAME	Acres	Description	CH	COMMENTS
1840	Drops from	These	LTLs		

1839 – 8 May 1839, in K&Q Co court" Lee Boulware, executor of **John Kidd Jr., deceased**, assignee of S. S. Gatewood, plaintiff, against George Hoskins and William B. Davis, defendants} [very difficult script to read]…the court ruled that the plaintiffs recover from the defendants $2,798.72, the penalty of the said bond with interest thereon at the rate of 6% from 7 January 1839 till paid, plus costs.[124]

1839 – John Kidd Sr., father of John Kidd Jr., signed his will on 15 May 1839 in K&Q Co. This lengthy document names among his heirs his two grandchildren Maria D. Kidd and John B. Kidd, the children of his **deceased son John Kidd** (who died in 1836). This will was proven in K&Q Co Court on 8 July 1839.[125]

JOHN KIDD (5), deceased by 1819

1819- This **John Kidd** appears for the first time on the K&Q LTLs in 1819 (see table below), at which time he is deceased. He is identifiable only by his land, 30 acres that lay 18 miles east or southeast of the Courthouse, which was taxed for nearly 40 years in the name of his estate, from 1819 to 1857, and then drops from the LTLs in 1858. The LTLs also contain the notation 'free Negroes" from 1819 to 1827. The significance of the initials (DC) is not known.

Year	NAME	Acres	Description	CH	COMMENTS
1819-1823	John Kidd, deceased	30	Eliz. McKendrie	18E	"free Negroes"
1824-1827	John Kidd Est.	30	Eliz. McKendrie	18SE	"free Negroes"
1828-1837	John Kidd Est.	30	Thos. Lumpkin	18E	"free negroes" no longer listed
1838-1840	John Kidd Est. (DC)	30	Thos. Lumpkin	18E	
1841	-	-	-	-	Page with Ks missing
1842	John Kidd Est. (DC)	30	John Lumpkin	18E	

---

[124] *K&Q Superior Court of Law & Chancery Records, 1831-1851*, p. 131, retrieved from FHL #32114, image 161. Scanned image of this document is available in the K&Q Source Documents folder and the K&Q Court records subfolder.

[125] The original will was lost with the other K&Q records. Fortunately, a certified copy was made at some point, and was passed down in the family of John Boulware Kidd, this John Kidd's grandson. It is now part of the Ellen Gertrude Tompkins Kidd papers, 1791-1998, Accession 52005. Personal papers collection, The Library of Virginia, Richmond, VA. Photographed and transcribed by RK there, July 2018.

Year	NAME	Acres	Description	CH	COMMENTS
1843-1849	John Kidd Est.	30	John R. Lumpkin Estate	18E	
1850	-	-	-	-	Page with Ks missing
1851-1857	John Kidd Est.	30	John R. Lumpkin Estate	18E	

Who was this deceased John Kidd with the notation "free Negroes" attached to his land?

We have two theories: either this John Kidd was white and had free Negroes living on his land after this death, or this John Kidd himself was a free black man who died with other free blacks living on his land. There was a significant number of free blacks with the surname of Kidd living in K&Q Co in the 1800s, including the two John Kidds, below.

JOHN KIDDs (2), free Black males in K&Q County in 1833

1833 – Two **John Kidds** appears on a list of free black individuals living in K&Q Co (see Appendix Two for the full list). The first John Kidd is listed on page 6 of the list, a farmer, living at New Church. Also listed as living at New Church are Sally Kidd, a farmer; William Kidd, a wood cutter; and Polly Kidd, a spinner. The second John Kidd is listed on page 8, no occupation given, living "on own land."[126]

One of these John Kidds is also found on the 1833 K&Q PPTL; he's the only free Negro listed on this year's PPTLs, unlike previous and later lists. His entry seems to indicate that he owned one horse, and that he owned a slave.
He doesn't appear on the K&Q PPTLs again until 1842.

1842 – A "John Kidd, free Negro," once again is found on the K&Q PPTL in this year, in a list of free Negroes appended to this PPTL; these separate lists do not have details.

JOHN KIDD(s) UNPLACED

1793 – In 1793, for one year only on the early tax lists, a second **John Kidd** appears on the K&Q PPTL.

John Kidd, a Major in the K&Q Militia, deceased by 2 Sept 1794

John Kidd, a Major in the K&Q Militia, deceased by 3 Jun 1799

[These entries may refer to the same person, but we do not know his identity.]

1794 – a **John Kidd** appears on a Militia List, dated 1793-1799, from the Archives Division, LOV, abstracted in Beverly Fleet's vol. 15 on K&Q Co: Fleet says it is headed "Numerical Rank

---

[126] Virginia. Auditor of Public Accounts (1776-1928). Free blacks records, 1833-1863. APA 757 1082990_0007_0004_0001_0011 Library of Virginia. This information can be found at "Virginia Untold: The African American Narrative," http://www.virginiamemory.com/collections/aan/.

Roll of the Field Officers of the Militia of Virginia….The following are marked as Majors and dated 2 Sept 1794: 359, **John Kidd**, deceased."[127]

1799 – in the same abstract, a John Kidd appears on a Militia List, King and Queen Co 9th Regiment, listed as "**John Kidd**, Major, 3 Jun 1799, deceased."[128]

John Kidd, a private in the militia in the War of 1812

1812-1814 - Private **John Kidd** is listed on the muster roll of Captain Thomas Faulkner's Company, 9th regiment. Time of service was 18 days.[129]

Private John Kidd is listed on the muster roll of Reubin Garnett's Company from the 9th Regiment, Virginia Militia, commanded by Lt. Col. William Boyd, from the 2nd of December to the 10th of December and from the 10th to the _ 1814. Wm. Stuart sub for J. Kidd. Time of service was 10 days.[130]

Private **John Kidd** was on the muster roll of Captain William Hutcherson's Company from the 9th Regiment, Virginia Militia, commanded by LT. Col. William Boyd from the 7th to the 17th of April 1813 and from the 2nd to the 10th of December 1814. Time of service was 10 days.

Also listed in this Company is Thomas Kidd. [131]

JOHN BOULWARE KIDD (1836-1910), the son of John (M.?) Kidd(4) and Catherine F. Boulware, grandson of John Kidd Sr. of K&Q Co and great-grandson of William Kidd Sr. of Caroline Co.
John7 (John6, John5, William4, Daniel3, Thomas2, Thomas1) Kidd
Born in 1836 in K&Q County
Moved from K&Q County to Richmond VA by 1860.
Twice married, first to Ann Roberta Tompkins, who likely died before 1875, and second to Gertrude Ellen Tompkins, Ann Roberta's sister.
Died 14 October 1910 in Richmond, Virginia.

There is extensive information about this family at the Library of Virginia in the papers of his wife Gertrude Ellen Tompkins Kidd, including photos of the family, their Richmond home, the Tompkins family, and her business achievements after his death.[132]

---

[127] *Virginia Colonial Abstracts*, vol. 15, Records of King and Queen Co, p. 57, by Beverley Fleet.

[128] Ibid., p. 86.

[129] "Virginia Militia in the War of 1812, vol. 2, from the rolls of the Auditor's Office", by Stuart Butler, page 318, located at LVA, viewed 7-17-2009, WRK.

[130] "Virginia Militia in the War of 1812, vol. 2, from the rolls of the Auditor's Office", by Stuart Butler, pages 348-349, located at LVA, viewed 7-17-2009, WRK.

[131] "A Guide to Virginia Militia Units in the War of 1812", by Stuart Lee Butler, pages 468-469, located at LVA, viewed 7-17-2009, WRK.

[132] Ellen Gertrude Tompkins Kidd papers, 1791-1998. Accession number 52005. Personal papers collection, Library of Virginia, Richmond, VA; viewed by RK July 2018. A summary of these records and an inventory of them are available on the LoV website, under Archives & Manuscripts.

Not dated -- In *King and Queen County, Virginia* by Rev. Alfred Bagby, 1908, p.366, in a section titled "Fragments", Bagby names "Kidd. – John Kidd Sr., lived near Munday's Bridge. Children: John, Mary (Bagby), Elizabeth (Motley and Bagby), John Jr., the father of **John B. Kidd**."[133]

1850 – on federal census in Drysdale Parish, K&Q Co., p. 200, HH 848:
    Boulware, Kiturah [Catherine] 63FW (no occupation listed) $4300 VA
    Broaddus, Caroline37FW VA
    Kidd, Catherine F. 36FW VA
    " , Maria Louisa 16FW VA
    " , **John B**. 14MW VA
    Broaddus, Wm. Lee 3MW VA
    Taliaferro, Catherine L. 8FW VA

1850s – **John B. Kidd** from K&Q was on a list of students at Richmond College "in the 1850s."[134]

1857 – "**J. Boulware Kidd** of King and Queen Co." married Ann Roberta, the daughter of E.W. Tompkins, of Richmond on July 29, 1857.[135]

1860 – on the federal census in Henrico Co. (Eastern division), VA, Richmond P.O., HH 324/306:
    Kidd, John B. 24MW farmer $6000/5100 VA
    " , A. Roberta 27FW   VA
    " , Julia B. 2FW VA
    " , Walter 6/12MW VA

1870 – on federal census in the Madison ward of Richmond, Henrico Co., VA (mis-indexed at Ancestry as RIDD), p. 21, HH 128/117:
    Kidd, John B. 34MW Grocer $6000/3000 VA
    " , Ann 35FW keeps house VA
    " , Julia 11FW at home VA attended school within the year
    " , Walter 10MW at home VA attended school within the year
    " , Malcolm? 9MW at home VA attended school within the year
    " , Donell 2MW at home VA
    Home?, Julia 40Fmulatto domestic servant VA cannot read or write
    " , Irving 20Mmulatto domestic servant VA cannot read or write
    Harrie?, Sue 12FB nurse VA cannot read or write

1880 – on the federal census in Richmond, VA, ED 83, sheet 20C, page 154, HH 116/191:
    Kidd, J.B. MW 44M grocery store VA VA VA
    " , Ellen FW 34M wife keeping house VA VA VA
    " , Miss Bertie 21FW dau VA VA VA
    " , Walter 20MW son VA VA VA
    " , Malcolm 19MW son VA VA VA
    " , Donald 12MW son attends school VA VA VA
    " , Lulu 5FW dau VA VA VA

---

[133] *King and Queen County, Virginia*, by Rev. Alfred Bagby, Regional Publishing Co., Baltimore, MD, 1973. (The original book was published in 1908.) This book is available online in the catalog at Familysearch.org and Ancestry.com.

[134] Bulletin of the King & Queen County Historical Society, No. 34, page 2.

[135] Library of Virginia card catalogue, citing the Richmond Whig & Public Advertiser, Tuesday, August 4, 1857. Scanned image in the K&Q County BD folder.

" , Carrie 2FW dau VA VA VA
" , unnamed infant WM 2/12 b. April VA VA VA
(this appears to be a multi-family dwelling, and next door appear to be several servants, probably for this Kidd family)

1900 – on the federal census in Richmond, Henrico Co., VA, ED 79, sheet 9B, living at 706 East Leigh St., HH 115/189:
Kidd, John B. WM Feb 1836 64M marr26yr VA VA VA Pickle business
" , Ellen B. wife WF Nov 1855 44M marr26yr VA VA VA Pickle mfg.
" , Marie L. dau WF Nov 1870 19 [should be 29] S VA VA VA
" , Allan son WM Jan 1882 18S VA VA VA at school
" , Caroline dau WF Aug 1883 16S VA VA VA at school
" , Leo son WM Oct. 1884 15S VA VA VA at school
" , Hugh son WM March 1886 14S VA VA VA at school

1910 – on the federal census in Richmond (Madison ward), an independent city within Henrico Co., VA, ED 110, sheet 9B, at the same address as in 1900:
Kidd, John B. WM 74M2 marr35yr VA VA VA Manufacturer, pickles
" , Ellen B. wife WF 50M1 marr35yr VA VA VA Manufacturer, pickles
" , Allan B. son WM 27S VA VA VA clerk, pickle factory
" , Leo son WM 25S VA VA VA clerk, pickle factory
" , Hugh T. son WM 24S VA VA VA secretary, pickle factory

John Boulware Kidd's obituary and funeral notice appeared in the *Richmond Times-Dispatch* on Sunday 16 Oct 1910, p. 2, nothing he had died on Friday 14 Oct:[136]

JOHN BOULWARE KIDD
Funeral services Will Take Place This Afternoon in Shockoe Hill Cemetery
John Boulware Kidd died at his residence, 706 East Leigh Street, Friday night in the seventy-fifth year of his age. He had not been in good health lately, but his death was unexpected. He was a man of wide acquaintance, having lived in Richmond nearly all his life, and was known for his conscientious spirit and his deeds of charity and kind words.
He was the son of John M. and Catherine Kidd, of King and Queen County, and nephew of William Boulware, United States Minister to Naples under President Tyler, and grandson of Colonel William S. Miller, a distinguished officer in the Revolutionary War. He was highly educated, and enjoyed the acquaintance of educators of distinction. He was a student of Richmond College and of Columbia University, and was sought as an authority in Greek, Latin and other classics.
Mr. Kidd was twice married. His last wife was Miss Ellen Tompkins, who survives him. He is also survived by eight children: Mrs. Burton Loomis[137], Walter Kidd, D.S. Kidd of New York; Mrs. E. Henry Meanley, of this City; Mrs. T.J. Foote, of Wilson, N.C.; and A.B., D.F. and H.T. Kidd. [Mrs. Burton Loomis was daughter Julia]

---

[136] Found on-line at America's GenealogyBank; scanned images in K&Q file.
[137] There is a woman named Burton K. Loomis on the federal census in NYC on the 1910 federal census. She's the wife of Ernest Loomis, an author and publisher. This entry lists her DOB as May 1863, and the birthplaces of her and both parents as Virginia. I believe that this is indeed John B.'s daughter, and that she's the Julia B. Kidd, actually born about 1858, judging from the 1860 census.

A subsequent brief news notice appeared in the *Richmond Times-Dispatch* on 22 Oct 1910, stating that John B. Kidd's wife, Ellen G. Kidd, qualified as the executor of his estate, valued at $18,000, and that all his property is bequeathed in fee simple to his widow.

John B. Kidd's widow, Ellen Gertrude Tompkins Kidd, died 3 Feb 1932 in Richmond. Her obituaries were published one and two days later, with information about her parents and her children.[138] Her 4 Feb obituary was on the front page of the *Richmond Times-Dispatch*.

A half-page article on Ellen and the pickle business she started appears in the *Richmond Times-Dispatch* on Sunday 11 Oct 1925. Its title was "Pickles Help Put Richmond on Business Map – How Old Colonial Recipe Brought Fame and Fortune To Virginian Woman Is Romance of Business World."
After her death, her estate was valued at over $400,000, less $150,000 in debts. Her surviving children (Leon M. Kidd, Hugh T. Kidd, Louise K. Meanley and Caroline K. Foote) sued the receivers of her estate, American Bank and Trust, and won an injunction against them in 1933.[139]

JOHN WESTLEY KIDD (b ca 1834, d July 1849)

1849 – A boy by this name died in July of 1849 in K&Q Co at the age of 15 years; cause of death is difficult to decipher but appears to be "dyspepsia" of 5 years' duration.[140] This record did not name his parents.

KITTY KIDD, a free black female in 1833

1833 -- **Kitty Kidd** appears on a list of free black individuals living in K&Q Co (see Appendix Two for the full list), listed on page 8, occupation spinner, noted as living "on own land."[141]

<u>LEWIS T. KIDD</u>, the son of Henry and Maria Bullock Kidd of Caroline Co VA.
Lewis T.7 (Henry6, Joel5, William4, Daniel3, Thomas2, Thomas1) Kidd
Born 3 March 1823 in Caroline Co VA.
Was a schoolteacher and ran a school at Newtown in K&Q Co.
Lived most of his life in Caroline County.
To our knowledge he never married.
Died 21 July 1896, likely in Caroline Co., VA.
Buried in Greenlawn Cemetery, Bowling Green, Caroline Co (as are four of his siblings William J., Benjamin F., Maria Louisa, and Betty Alice Kidd).

---

[138] Richmond Times-Dispatch, Friday, Feb. 5, 1932, p. 24 (scan in K&Q file).

[139] Ellen Gertrude Tompkins Kidd papers, 1791-1998. Accession number 52005. Personal papers collection, Library of Virginia, Richmond, VA; viewed by RK July 2018. A summary of these records and an inventory of them are available on the LoV website, under Archives & Manuscripts.

[140] the 1850 federal census mortality schedule for K&Q Co, available online at Familysearch.org.

[141] Virginia. Auditor of Public Accounts (1776-1928). Free blacks records, 1833-1863. APA 757 1082990_0007_0004_0001_0011 Library of Virginia. This information can be found at "Virginia Untold: The African American Narrative," http://www.virginiamemory.com/collections/aan/.

1843-1850 – **Lewis T. Kidd** first appears on the **Caroline Co VA** PPTLs in 1843, and appears annually thereafter through 1850, but not thereafter (through 1855, the last year we have checked).

Year	Taxpayer	WMT	B> 16	B 12 -16	H	COMMENTS
1843	Lewis T. Kidd	1	0	0	1	
1844	Lewis T. Kidd	1	0	0	1	
1845	Lewis T. Kidd	1	0	0	1	
1846	Lewis T. Kidd	1	0	0	1	Patent lever or lepine silver watch
1847	Lewis T. Kidd	1	0	0	1	
1848	Lewis T. Kidd	1	0	0	1	
1849	Lewis T. Kidd	1	0	0	0	1 patent lever watch
1850	Lewis T. Kidd	1	0	0	0	1 patent lever watch
1851	Falls from lists					

1850 – **Lewis T. Kidd** is on the federal census in Caroline Co VA, p. 271A, HH 738/739:
Puller, Rich'd A. 23WM farmer $800 VA
  " , Sarah A. 16FW (all birthplace entries below Richard's are blank)
  " , Genevieve 6/12FW
  " , Catherine 60FW $1000
Broaddus, Harvey M. 12MW
Kidd, Lewis T. 27MW Teacher
Broaddus, Eugene L. 10MW
Puller, James E. 16MW student

1851, 1853-1855 – In each of these years, a **Lewis T. Kidd** appears on the annual **K&Q** PPTLs, taxed only for himself.

1853-1860 – **Lewis T. Kidd** first appears on the K&Q LTLs in 1853, taxed upon 1 acre 28 miles NW of the Courthouse. The description of his land states "New Town," and he acquired it by deed from "B__ Gresham" in the prior few months.
This entry repeats annually through 1860, and in that year, his residence is listed as "South Carolina."

1860 – According to his LTL entries (above), he was evidently residing in South Carolina in 1860; we found no census record for him in either Virginia or South Carolina.

1861 – According to the K&Q LTL for 1861, **Lewis Kidd** transferred his 1 acre to Benjamin F. Gresham in that year, and he ceases to appear on the K&Q LTLs. He appears in the Caroline County 1870 and 1880 censuses and died in 1896.

1870 – On the federal census in Port Royal township, **Caroline County**, Virginia, Rappahannock Academy P. O., page 349, HH 419/433, living with his brother, William and William's wife. Also in the HH is their mother, Maria.
Kidd, Wm 45MW Farmer $1350/275 VA

     " , Fannie 38FW housekeeper VA
     " , Lewis   47MW schoolteacher VA
     " , Maria   69FW no occupation VA
Bullock, Alice 72FW no occupation VA
Kidd, Frank B. 36MW dentist VA
     " , Louise 30FW at home VA
     " , Alice 22FW at home VA
Rollins, Thom 10MB domestic VA

1880 – On the federal census in Port Royal township, Caroline County, Virginia, page 26B, HH 253/283:

     Kidd, Lewis T. WM 57S   head   Farmer VA VA VA
     " , Wm. J. WM 55S brother Farmer VA VA VA
     " , Maria L. WF 39S sister Teacher VA VA VA
     " , Alice B. WF 33S sister at home VA VA VA
Bullock, Alice T. WF 82S aunt   VA VA VA
Beverly, Francis BF 23S domestic servant VA VA VA
     " , William H. BM 10/12S b. August VA VA VA

1896 – According to his headstone in the Greenlawn Cemetery in Bowling Green, Caroline County, Virginia, **Lewis T. Kidd** was born on 3 March 1823 and died on 21 July 1896. A brief biography on Findagrave says that he served in the 6th Virginia Infantry, CSA, and that he was the brother of William J., Maria L., and Alice Betty Kidd, and nephew of Alice T. Bullock. He apparently never married.

LOUISA KIDD, a free Black female in 1833

1833 – **Louisa Kidd** appears on a list of free black individuals living in K&Q Co (see Appendix Two for the full list), listed on page 8, noted as living "on own land."[142]

LUCY KIDD(s)

LUCY KIDD, wife of Thomas Lambeth of Middlesex County, Virginia

1786 – **Lucy Kidd** of King and Queen Co. married Thomas Lambeth of Middlesex Co on 18 Oct. 1786, according to *Some Marriages in the Burned Record Counties of Virginia*, by the Virginia Genealogical Society, 1972.[143]

Lucy Kidd (of King and Queen) married a Thomas Lambeth on 18 October of this year. At the end of page 205 of the CCP Register is written: "The above drawn off for the Clerks of those County's wherein the above Marriages were solemnized." Kidd marriages listed on page 205 are Benjamin Kidd to Mary Guthrie dated 1784, and three dated 1786: William Kidd to Rachel Chowning, Lucy Kidd (King and Queen) to Thomas Lambeth, and Henry

---

[142] Virginia. Auditor of Public Accounts (1776-1928). Free blacks records, 1833-1863. APA 757 1082990_0007_0004_0001_0011 Library of Virginia. This information can be found at "Virginia Untold: The African American Narrative," http://www.virginiamemory.com/collections/aan/.

[143] Page 62, citing the Christ Church Parish Register, p. 265.

Kidd to Catherine Swords [Seward]. However, only the notations for Mary Guthrie and Lucy Kidd say King and Queen specifically.[144]

LUCY KIDD, wife of John Kidd (1)

1801 – **Lucy Kidd,** John Kidd's widow, appears on the K&Q PPTL in 1801, the year after John Kidd drops from these annual PPTLs with no white male tithes in her HH. She has the same number of slaves that John Kidd (1) did in 1800; see his section of this work for more details.

YEAR	TAXPAYER	WT	B>16	B 12 -16	H	COMMENTS
1801	Lucy	0	8	1	3	Wm Fleet's list

She drops from the PPTLs in 1802 and does not reappear.

1801 – 16 June 1801, **Essex County** court. **Lucy Kidd**, executrix of **John Kidd, deceased**, Petitioner against Thomas Dix and John Croxton, Defendants} On Petition Defendants though solemnly called failed to appear…Court rules that the petitioner recover of the defendants the sum of £4.5.2, and also her costs…the defendants in mercy, etc…this Judgment is to be discharged by the payment of £1.2 with interest from 1 January 1794 till payment, and her costs.[145]

It is possible that some of the free Negroes living in K&Q Co were among the slaves of John Kidd (1) and his wife Lucy. We base this upon the K&Q PPTLs for this John Kidd between 1783 and 1786 in the table below. The names of at least six of the slaves of John Kidd (1) on the 1783-1786 PPTLs match those individuals who appear as free Negroes in the 1813 PPTLs, some 30 years later; Frank, Hannah, Humphrey, James, Sally (variously listed as Sally, Sall and Sarah) and Sam Kidd appear on both lists. And John's slave named Will *could* be the same individual as the free Negro Billy Kidd on the 1813 PPTL. Moreover, of these, all but James and Hannah were under the age of 16 in 1783-1786. While the gap of 30 years and the fact that there may have been other slaves with these given names must be considered, it is possible that John, Lucy, or one of their heirs freed their slaves.

YEAR	TAXPAYER	WT	B>16	B<16	H	Cattle	COMMENTS
1782	John	1	4	7	3	17	slaves not named
1783	John	1	3	6	4	15	8 others listed by name: Lucy,[146] James, Molley, Hannah, Sally, Sam, Frank, &

---

[144] *Parish Register of Christ Church Parish, Middlesex Co., Virginia, 1635-1812*, p 205.

[145] Essex County Order Book 36, page 154.

[146] This particular entry is perplexing because of a column heading - # of White Souls- that occurs in this single year, and which listed 2 white souls for John Kidd. We know from other records that his wife's given name was Lucy, and we believe that she is the Lucy in this record, and the second white tithe, in addition to John.

						Will; only 3 over 16. "2 White Souls"
1784	John	1	3	5	3	15	8 named slaves: James, Molley, Hannah, >16; Humphrey, Sall, Frank, Tom & Will <16.
1785	John	1	3	5	3	17	Slaves James, Milly, Hannah, Humphrey, Sarah, Peter, Frank & Sam
1786	John	1	4	5	2	16	Slaves James, Humphrey, Hannah, Milly, Peter, Sary, Frank, Sam, Will
1787	John	1	5	4	2	15	slaves not named in 1787 or thereafter

LUCY KIDD, a free black female in 1833

1833 – **Lucy Kidd** appears on a list of free black individuals living in K&Q Co (see Appendix Two for the full list), listed on page 8, noted as living "on own land."[147]

MARIA KIDD UPSHAW, daughter of John Kidd(3) of K&Q County
Probably born by 1799
Married James Upshaw, place uncertain[148]
Died before 1839 (see below)

1826 – Married on 15 Ult.[Jan] by Rev. Thomas M. Henley, Dr. James W. Upshaw of Caroline Co., to Miss Maria Kidd, daughter of Mr. **John Kidd** of King & Queen Co.[149] Another abstract shows the groom's name as "Mr. John Upshur."[150]

1830 – On the federal census in Caroline County, Virginia:
James Upshaw – 2WM 5-9 and 1 WM 50-59; 1WF under 5 and 1 WF 30-39. 6 slaves. This record most likely belongs to this couple, and if so indicates that the two young males likely were from an earlier wife, and not Maria's children [see next record].

1839 – In his will written in 1839, John Kidd(3) names among his heirs "my three grandchildren, James M.D. Upshaw, Thomas E. Upshaw and Sarah Ann Upshaw," giving them a share of his estate equal to that given to his surviving daughter, Mary Ann Bagby, and to the children

---

[147] Virginia. Auditor of Public Accounts (1776-1928). Free blacks records, 1833-1863. APA 757 1082990_0007_0004_0001_0011 Library of Virginia. This information can be found at "Virginia Untold: The African American Narrative," http://www.virginiamemory.com/collections/aan/.

[149] *Marriages and Deaths from Richmond, Virginia Newspapers 1780-1820*. Special Publication No. 8. Richmond, VA: Virginia Historical Society, 1983, p. 181, citing the *Richmond Enquirer*, 19 Jan 1826, p. 3 (from Craig Kilby).

[150] *Marriage Notices from Richmond, Virginia Newspapers 1821-1840*. Special Publication No. 10. Richmond, VA: Virginia Genealogical Society, 1988, p. 181, citing the *Richmond Examiner*, 19 Jan 1826, p. 3.

of his deceased son John. This indicates that their mother Maria has died by 1839.[151] See John Kidd(3) section.

MARIA KIDD, a free black female in 1833

1833 – **Maria Kidd** appears on a list of free black individuals living in K&Q Co (see Appendix Two for the full list), listed on page 6, along with Sarah, Polly, Elizabeth, and James Kidd, noted as living on Paul Philpot's land. This may indicate they were a family in the same household.[152]

MARIA LOUISA KIDD (~1834-1853), the daughter of John Kidd(4) and his wife Catherine F. Boulware

1850 – on federal census in Drysdale Parish, K&Q Co, p. 200, HH 848:
    Boulware, Kiturah [Catherine] 63FW (no occupation listed) $4300 VA
    Broaddus, Caroline 37FW VA
    Kidd, Catherine F. 36FW VA
    " , **Maria Louisa** 16FW VA
    " , John B. 14MW VA
    Broaddus, Wm. Lee 3MW VA
    Taliaferro, Catherine L. 8FW VA

1853 – **Maria L. Kidd** died in K&Q Co. "Expired on the 5th instant [i.e. 5 Mar 1853] at New Town, King & Queen, **Maria Louisa Kidd**, of a long protracted illness." [153]

MARY ANN KIDD , the daughter of John Kidd(3) and his wife Ann (possibly Lumpkin)
Born 3 November 1809
Married Travis Bagby in 1834, most likely in K&Q
Died 17 Oct 1874 in Caroline Co VA

Not dated -- In *King and Queen County, Virginia* by Rev. Alfred Bagby, 1908, p.366, in a section titled "Fragments", Bagby names "Kidd. – John Kidd Sr., lived near Munday's Bridge. Children: John, **Mary (Bagby)**, Elizabeth (Motley and Bagby), John Jr., the father of John B. Kidd."[154]

---

[151] [151] The original will was lost with the other K&Q records. Fortunately, a certified copy was made at some point, and was passed down in the family of John Boulware Kidd, this John Kidd's grandson. It is now part of the Ellen Gertrude Tompkins Kidd papers, 1791-1998, Accession 52005. Personal papers collection, The Library of Virginia, Richmond, VA. Photographed and transcribed by RK there, July 2018.

[152] Virginia. Auditor of Public Accounts (1776-1928). Free blacks records, 1833-1863. APA 757 1082990_0007_0004_0001_0011 Library of Virginia. This information can be found at "Virginia Untold: The African American Narrative," http://www.virginiamemory.com/collections/aan/.

[153] Pippenger, Wesley E. *Death Notices from Richmond, Virginia Newspapers 1841-1853*. Richmond, VA: Virginia Genealogical Society, 2002. These are arranged chronologically, with an every-name index, p. 426, citing the *Richmond Enquirer*, 25 Mar 1853, p. 2.

[154] *King and Queen County, Virginia*, by Rev. Alfred **Bagby**, Regional Publishing Co., Baltimore, MD, 1973. (The original book was published in 1908.) This book is available online in the catalog at Familysearch.org and Ancestry.com.

1809 -- **Mary Ann Kidd** was born 3 November 1809, according to the Bagby Family Bible.[155]

1834 – On 28 January 1834, **Mary Ann Kidd** and Travis Bagby were married, most likely in K&Q Co.[156]

1838 – Ann Kidd of K&Q County wrote and signed her will on 20 May 1838. In it, she named the children of her two sisters, Elizabeth and Mary Ann, and any unborn children, as her heirs.[157] At the time the will was written, Elizabeth's name was Elizabeth Bagby, and she had four daughters: Ann Elizabeth Motley, Mary Frances Motley and Andrewetta Motley, and Virginia Bagby. **Mary Ann Bagby's**[158] children were John Richard Bagby, Ann Elizabeth Bagby, and an unborn child at the writing of Ann Kidd's will, but who was subsequently named Travis Bagby (apparently after his father and Mary Ann's husband, since Mr. Travis Bagby, "my brother-in-law," was named Ann Kidd's executor).
Her will also bequeaths $300 to "Mr. Kidd" for caring for her while she was sick, but doesn't record his given name. Her will was admitted into court in October 1838.[159]

1839 – On 8 Nov 1839, a suit in Chancery court was heard in K&Q Co for the division of the estate of Ann Kidd. The purpose of the suit was to divide the estate between the children of Ann's sisters Elizabeth and Mary Ann, to establish the inheritance of Travis, the youngest child of Mary Ann Kidd Bagby (she was pregnant at the time of her sister Ann's death), and to make a division of Ann Kidd's slaves.

In a Court held for K&Q County on Friday 8 Nov 1839:
Ann Elizabeth Motley, Mary Frances Motley, Andrewetta Motley and Virginia Bagby, children of Elizabeth Bagby; John Richard Bagby, Ann Elizabeth Bagby and Travis Bagby, children of **Mary Ann Bagby**, all of whom are infants under the age of twenty one years, by John Bagby their next friend, Pltfs.
against
Travis Bagby Executor of Ann Kidd, deceased, Deft. } In Chancery

This cause came on this day by consent of parties to be heard upon the bill and answer, and the will of Ann Kidd filed as [one?] exhibit in the cause and was argued by counsel, upon consideration whereof the Court being of the opinion that the devises or bequests contained

---

[155] Bagby Family Bible (1750-1860), Virginia Historical Society Acc. Mss6:4 B1465:1. A transcription of this bible is found in *Bible Records of Caroline County, Virginia Families*, by Herbert Ridgeway Collins, Heritage Books, Westminster, MD, 2008, pp. 10-ff. A <u>card index</u> for this (and many other Virginia family Bibles) is available at www.familysearch.org/search/collection/1932510

[156] Ibid.

[157] Lost Records Localities Digital Collection, King and Queen County, Kidd, Ann will, 1838. Library of Virginia, Richmond, VA 23219. This will can be seen online at http://www.virginiamemory.com/collections/lost and then searching on "Kidd."

[158] Mary A. Bagby died 17 Oct 1874 in Caroline Co., VA at the age of 64, according to Virginia Deaths and Burials, 1853-1917 at Ancestry.com. Her death record lists her spouse as Travis Bagby, and names her parents as "John and Ann Kidd" (citing FHL #2056976).

[159] King & Queen Chancery Cause 1840-001, online at: http://www.lva.virginia.gov/chancery/case_detail.asp?CFN=097-1840-001 . An abstract of this estate record is available from RK (now stored in the K&Q shared folder). This will and chancery suit also cited in *Index to Virginia Estates, 1800-1865*, vol. 10, compiled by Wesley E. Pippenger, published by Virginia Genealogical Society, 2010.

in the said will to the future children of Testatrix' two sisters, Elizabeth Bagby and **Mary Ann Bagby** who was *in ventre sa mere*[160] at the death of the said Testatrix

and that the estate devised or bequeathed by the said Testatrix to the children which her said sisters then had and might thereafter have vested in the children which the Testatrix's said sisters had living at the time of her death and in the said infant *in ventre sa mere*, doth therefore adjudge order and decree that the estate of Ann Kidd deceased be divided first into moieties [shares], and that one moiety be divided into four equal parts and the Court doth decree one of said four parts to each of the plaintiffs Elizabeth Motley, Mary Francis Motley, Andrewetta Motley and Virginia Bagby and that James M. Jeffries, John Bagby and Richard Bagby as commissioners for the purpose hereby appointed do fairly value the slaves of the estate of said Ann Kidd and make division of them as herein before ordered

and that in said case the said commissioners shall find that the required divisions cannot be made of the slaves in kind, that after advertising the time and place for thirty days at several of the most public places in the neighborhood, they sell one or more of the slaves as the may find necessary upon a credit of six months except as to the expenses of the sale, which they may require in cash, and that they take bonds with good security payable to such of the said parties and for such sums as will affect the required divisions and that the slaves and bonds be delivered to the guardians of those respectively entitled to them and that they report to Court their proceedings herein, and that the Defendant pay over to the guardians of the said Elizabeth Bagby's children their respective proportions of the funds in his hands. As to the other moiety of the estate, the use thereof being bequeathed by the Testatrix to the Defendant for the term of five years, the Court doth not make any order in relation thereto at this time, and this cause is retained for future proceedings. The Court doth further order that the effect of this decree be so far suspended, that the parties or their guardians shall not be entitled to receive their portions of the estate until the Defendant shall be properly indemnified by refunding bonds if he require it. The Court doth further adjudge, order and decree that the Defendant as Exer. of said Ann Kidd do pay the costs of this suit.[161] [162]

1840 – On the federal census in Caroline Co VA, page 76, line 16:
Travis Bagby: 2M<5 & 1 30-39; 1F 5-9,1 F 10-14, 1 F 40-49 AND 1 F 80-89.
The elderly female could be the mother of Travis, or of Mary Ann.

Travis Bagby is also found on the 1840 federal census in K&Q Co VA, page 86, line 5; his entry lists him as "Travis Bagby Exr. Jno. Kidd." This household includes 2M 10-15 and 1 F 20-29; and 1F 40-49, along with 23 slaves. Ten in Agriculture. This unusual entry is John Kidd(3)'s estate, with his wife and children.

1841 – In a Court held for K&Q Co on 5 May 1841.
Ann Elizabeth Motley, Mary Francis Motley, Andrewetta Motley and Virginia Bagby children of Elizabeth Bagby; John Richard Bagby, Ann Elizabeth Bagby and Travis Bagby, children

---

[160] A French law term meaning "in the womb of its mother." Mary Ann was pregnant when her sister Ann died.

[161] King & Queen Chancery Cause 1840-001, online at:
http://www.lva.virginia.gov/chancery/case_detail.asp?CFN=097-1840-001 . An abstract of this estate record is available from RK (now stored in the K&Q shared folder). This will and chancery suit also cited in *Index to Virginia Estates, 1800-1865*, vol. 10, compiled by Wesley E. Pippenger, published by Virginia Genealogical Society, 2010.

[162] King & Queen Co. Order Book, 1831-1851 (LoV reel #8), reviewed by RK July 24, 2018, p. 89. Scanned images available from the authors.

of **Mary Ann Bagby**, all of whom are infants under the age of twenty one years by John Bagby their next friend, Plts.

against

Travis Bagby, executor of Ann Kidd, dec'd., Deft }In Chancery

This cause came on this day to be again heard on the papers formerly Read and the report of Commissioners having been returned more than one month and no exception having been taken thereto, it is ordered that the same be confirmed.[163]

1849 – Mary Ann's husband Travis Bagby died on 1 December 1849, "in the 49th year of his age," according to his headstone in the Bagby family cemetery in Lauraville, Caroline Co VA.[164]

1850 – On the federal census in Caroline Co VA, page 270 HH 732/733:

Mary A. Bagby 40FW $5,000 real estate VA
Ann E.   "   14FW VA attended school within the year
Travis   "   12MW VA attended school within the year
Thomas G. "   10MW VA attended school within the year
Mary L.   "   3FW VA
Sallie M.   "   1FW VA

1860 – On the federal census in Caroline County, Virginia, Sparta P.O., page 93, HH 104:

Travis **Bagby** 22MW farmer $0/3000 VA
Mary A. "   50FW $6000/10,000 VA
Thomas G. "   19MW $0/3300 VA
Mary L.   "   13FW $4000 VA

1870 - On the federal census in Bowling Green, Caroline County, Virginia, page 330, HH 279/290:

Bagby, Travis   32MW farmer $7000 real estate/$400 personal est. VA
" , **Mary A.**   60FW keeping house no real or personal estate
Butler, Ann E. 33FW $500/150   VA
" , Lizzie O. 12FW VA
" , Edward E. 14MW VA

1874 – **Mary A. Bagby** died 17 Oct 1874 in Caroline Co VA at the age of 64.[165] Her death record lists her spouse as Travis Bagby (1800-1849), and names her parents as "John and Ann Kidd".

She is buried in the Bagby family cemetery in Lauraville, Caroline Co VA along with her husband, Travis Bagby, and several of their children.[166]

MARY KIDD – found in early K&Q Co merchant record in 1750-1751

1750-1751 – a **Mary Kidd** is recorded in Merchants' Ledgers of **K&Q Co**. On p 115, the account of John Sutton: **Mary Kidd**, pr yr [prior year?] order 13 bushalls salt, 26 p.[167]

---

[163] King & Queen Co. Order Book, 1831-1851 (LoV reel #8), reviewed by RK July 24, 2018, p. 107. Scanned image available upon request.

[164] See Findagrave.com: www.findagrave.com/memorial/83799532/travis-bagby

[165] "Virginia Deaths and Burials, 1853-1917" at Ancestry.com, citing FHL #2056976.

[166] See Findagrave.com: https://www.findagrave.com/memorial/152124435

[167] From Virginia Genealogical Society Quarterly, citing Book A, p 88, Book B p 126, Book C, p 212.

MOLLEY KIDD –in K&Q Co in 1788

1788 – **Molley Kidd** appears on the membership list (p. 10 of the minute book) for Upper King and Queen Baptist Church, listed as "Dismist." Directly above Molley Kidd's name appears that of Fanny Kidd, listed as "Dismist." Other Kidd individuals mentioned in these church records are Edmund Kidd, John Kidd, William Kidd, Sr. and William Kidd Jr.[168]
She may be the Mary/Molly Kidd above, or the one below.

MARY/MOLLY KIDD – a K&Q Co head of household in 1810-1820

1810 – on federal census in K&Q Co., p. 222B, line 7
Mary Kidd – no males; 2F 16-25 & 1 45 and up. No slaves.

1820 – on federal census in K&Q Co., Stratton Major Parish
Molly Kidd – 1F 26-44 & 1 45 and up; no slaves.

MOSES KIDD, son of William and Margaret Kidd of Middlesex County, Virginia
**Moses3 (William2, Thomas1) Kidd
Baptized 30 Mar 1707 in MSX Co VA
Married Dorothy [maiden name unknown].
One known daughter, Martha, born 7 May 1739 and baptized 4 June 1739 in Middlesex Christ Church Parish.
One known son (name not given), named as chain carrier with Moses ["Moses and son"] in a 1752 King & Queen Co record (see below).**

**Moses Kidd left Middlesex Co in the years following his parents' 1727 deaths, traveling in the same timeframe and direction as several of his siblings.
Moses is the first Kidd found in the records of Caroline County, preceding his siblings James (1741), Duel (1743), Aaron (1747) and John (1751).
A handful of records for Moses have been found in Caroline and King & Queen Counties, and <u>all known mentions of him are included here</u>.**

No proven living descendants have been found as of September 2020.

1707 – **Moses Kidd** was baptized 30 Mar 1707 in **MSX Co VA** as the son of William and Margaret Kidd.[169]

1733/4 – At a **Caroline** County court held 14 Mar 1733/4: Thomas Carr acknowledged his deeds of lease and release of land indented to **Moses Kidd**.[170]

On the same court date—14 Mar 1733/4—the will of Michael Nailing is presented to the court by Rebecca Nailing and Robert Fleming, Gent. **Moses Kidd** and John Scott witnesses.[171]

---

[168] *Upper King and Queen Baptist Church Records, King and Queen County, 1774-1788*, transcribed by Richard Slatten and Edgar MacDonald, published in Virginia Genealogical Society *Quarterly*, vol. 30, no. 1, p. 64, February 1992.
[169] Christ Church Parish Register.
[170] *Caroline Co. VA Order Book part 1, 1732-1734/5*, abstracted and compiled by John Frederick Dorman, Washington, DC, 1965, pp. 129.
[171] Caroline County VA Order Book 1732-1740, pp. 131.

1737 – At a **Caroline** County court held 13 May 1737: **Moses Kid** (sic) acknowledged his deeds of lease and release of land indented to William Ballard. [deed of lease and release is fee simple].[172]

1738 – Moses also had at least one son, whose name is unknown, but who likely was born by 1738. This son presumably was at least 14 when he was identified in a 1752 K&Q record that named **Moses Kidd** "and son" as chain carriers (see 1752, below).

1739 – **Moses Kidd** and wife Dorothy had at least one child named in the CCP Register, named Martha, born 7 May 1739 and baptized 4 June 1739.[173]

1747 - **Moses Kidd** is named in a small hand-made book, a rent book of William Beverley of Blandfield, containing the names of 119 tenants on his various estates. Rents were paid principally in tobacco or wool. The book is marked "Rents due on the 27th of Nov. 1747. Among the tenants at "Beverley Park" in **K&Q Co**. was **Moses Kidd**.[174]

1750-1751 – a **Moses Kidd** has three separate entries in Merchants' Ledgers of K&Q Co. during this time span.[175] One of them indicates that he was charged for "one Parish levy."

1752 – The 1752 Account Book of William Beverley, the very wealthy landowner in K&Q County cited above, contained one more mention of Moses Kidd and his son (who was not named): "**Moses Kidd**, resident tenant of Beverley Park, King & Queen Co VA: to this year's rent of 574 pounds, credit issued in 1753 for services: "by yourself & son carrying [th]e [surveyors] chain in ful[l] 574 [lbs]".[176]

WE HAVE FOUND NO FURTHER RECORDS FOR THIS MOSES KIDD.

MOSES KIDD, a free black carpenter

1813-1849 – A free Negro named **Moses Kidd** appears on many of the K&Q PPTLs between 1813 and 1849, shown in the table below.

Moses and Sam Kidd were listed frequently on the K&Q PPTLs with the white taxpayers (as opposed to appearing on separate lists of free Negroes), whereas the other free Negroes were more often listed only on a separate list for that year.

YEAR	TAXPAYER	NOTATION	COMMENTS
1813	Moses Kidd	"free Negro"	Dist. Of Benj. Faulkner
1814	Moses Kidd	"free Negro"	Dist. Of John W. Fleet
1816	Moses Kidd	"free Negro"	Dist. Of Francis Row
1818	Moses Kidd	"free Negro"	List of Francis Row; separate list of "Free Negroes & Mulattos" end of this list.
1820	Moses Kidd	"free Negro"	List of Francis Row; separate list of "Free Negroes & Mulattos" end of this list.

---

[172] *Ibid.*, p. 415.

[173] *Christ Church Parish Register*, p. 134.

[174] *Virginia Colonial abstracts*, volume 4, by Beverley Fleet, p. 93.

[175] Virginia Genealogical Society Quarterly, citing Book A, p 81, Book B p 8, Book C, p 104.

[176] "Account Book of William Beverley, 1752," transcribed by John M. Weisner, citing page 20 of the account book, appearing in *Virginia Genealogical Society Quarterly*, vol. 41, pages 5-17. This mention is on page 11 of this volume. See also *Virginia Genealogical Society Quarterly*, vol. 41, pages 193, which corrected an omission in the earlier article.

1826	Moses Kidd	"free Negro"	A separate list of other FNs found at the end of the main list.
1836	Moses Kidd	"free Negro"	Only one on this list
1837	Moses Kidd	"free Negro"	Only one on this list
1838	Moses Kidd	"free Negro"	
1839	Moses Kidd	"free Negro"	List of John Pollard ; separate at end
1840	Moses Kidd	"free Negro"	List of John Pollard; with W polls
1841	Moses Kidd	"free Negro"	List of John Pollard; with W polls
1842	Moses Kidd	"free Negro"	List of John Pollard; with W polls
1843	Moses Kidd	"free Negro"	List of John Pollard; with W polls
1844	Moses Kidd	"free Negro"	List of John Pollard; with W polls; no separate list in 1844
1845	Moses Kidd	"free Negro"	List of John Pollard; with W polls; no separate list in 1845
1846	Moses Kidd	"free Negro"	List of John Pollard; with W polls; no separate list in 1846
1847	Moses Kidd	"free Negro"	List of John Pollard; with W polls; no separate list in 1847
1848	Moses Kidd	"free Negro"	List of John Pollard; with W polls; no separate list in 1848
1849	Moses Kidd	"free Negro"	List of John Pollard; with W polls

1830 – we do not find him on the 1830 federal census in K&Q.

1833 – **Moses Kidd** appears on a list of free black individuals living in K&Q Co (see Appendix Two for the full list), listed on page 8, occupation carpenter, living near Centerville.[177]

1840 – **Moses Kidd** appears on the K&Q Co census (p 107), Moses is listed alone as 1 free colored male, aged 36-54, engaged in manufacture and trade.

1850 – we do not find him on the 1850 federal census in K&Q or elsewhere and have found no further records for him.

NANCY KIDD(s) – See also ANN KIDD(s)
There are 4 women named Nancy Kidd found in K&Q records:
1. **NANCY KIDD (1), the wife of Benjamin(3) Kidd**
2. **NANCY KIDD (2), the daughter of Benjamin(3) Kidd and his wife Nancy(1)**
3. **NANCY KIDD, free Negro in K&Q, 1833**

---

[177] Virginia. Auditor of Public Accounts (1776-1928). Free blacks records, 1833-1863. APA 757 1082990_0007_0004_0001_0011 Library of Virginia. This information can be found at "Virginia Untold: The African American Narrative," http://www.virginiamemory.com/collections/aan/.

4. **NANCY S. KIDD, plaintiff in an 1835 Chancery suit (that also names her sisters Poly Kidd Brown and Harriet Kidd Walton.**

NANCY KIDD (1), the wife of Benjamin(3) Kidd, and the mother of Benjamin F., Richard, Nancy (Ann), William (W.S.), and likely Patsey (who married Thomas Hart)
Born abt. 1783 in Virginia[178]
Died in June 1855 of "old age"

1816 – a **Nancy Kidd** first appears on the K&Q PPTLs in 1816, with no white male tithes. This is the year following the death of Benjamin Kidd(3), and she appears to be his widow. She's listed annually through 1818, then drops from these lists.

1850 – on federal census in K&Q Co, St. Stephen's Parish, p. 161A, HH 197, living with her sons Richard and William and daughter Nancy(2):

Kidd, Richard 35MW farmer $400 VA
  " , **Nancy** 67FW   VA
  " , Nancy 42FW VA
  " , William 17MW laborer VA

1853-1855 – **Nancy Kidd** appears on the K&Q PPTLs in 1853, the year that Richard Kidd drops from the lists, with one white male tithe in her household (this would be son William, above).
In 1854, she has no white male tithes on her PPTL entry. In 1855, **Nancy's Kidd estate** is listed on the K&Q PPTLs, and she's died in the past 12 months.
See Table below:

YEAR	NAME	WM >16	B >16	WM >21	B >12	H	COMMENTS
1853	Nancy	1	0	0	0	0	12 cows, sheep, hogs (CSH)
1854	Nancy	0	0	0	2	0	10 CSH
1855	Nancy Est.	0	0	0	2	0	10 CSH

1855 – **Nancy Kidd**, a 65-year-old White female died of "old age" in June 1855 in K&Q County, Virginia.[179] The informant was "Rd. Whayne(?), Admr."

NANCY/ANN KIDD (2), the daughter of Benjamin(3) and Nancy(1) Kidd, and sister of Benjamin F., Richard, William (W.S.), and likely Patsey (who married Thomas Hart)
Born abt 1808, most likely in K&Q
Never married
Died testate in K&Q prior to 7 February 1862, when her will was admitted to Court

---

[178] Judging from her entry on the 1850 federal census, at which time she was 67 years old. However, the 1855 death record we have attributed to her (and which matches her K&Q PPTL entries) lists her age at death as 65 years, which calculates to a birth year of about 1790.

[179] Virginia Deaths and Burials Index, 1853-1917 at Ancestry.com, citing FHL # 2048575. This record is viewable on familysearch.org, FHL#2048575, image 264 of 673. Unfortunately the columns for her birthplace and the names of her parents were left blank.

1840 – on federal census in K&Q Co VA, p. 101:
Nancy Kidd – 1M 5-9 & 2 20-29; **1F 30-39**. One free Negro male 10-23 and two slaves (a male less than 10 and a female, 36-54). Three in agriculture. The adult whites could not read or write.

1850 – on federal census in K&Q Co, St. Stephen's Parish, p. 161A, HH 197:
Kidd, Richard 35MW farmer $400 VA
  " , Nancy 67FW   VA
  " , **Nancy** 42FW VA
  " , William 17MW laborer VA

1860 – on federal census in K&Q Co, Carlton's Store P.O., p. 74, HH 601:
Kidd, William 26MW day laborer $50/25 VA cannot read or write
HH 602
Kidd, Nancy 50FW weaver $300/170 VA cannot read or write
(nearby, HH 605 is a John H. Thurston, who was a neighbor of Benjamin Kidd)

[Note: this William is the W.S. Kidd who died by 1863 without heirs, whose inheritance of 8 acres from Nancy's will then goes to Richard Kidd and Dorothy Hart.]

1860-1862 – an **Ann Kidd**[180] first appears on the K&Q Land Tax Lists (LTLs) in 1860, when she's taxed upon 8 acres "adjoining the Benjamin Kidd Estate" 9 miles NE of the Courthouse. The notation reads, "Transferred from Benjamin Kidd's estate being sold by William Bird commissioner, being Benjamin Kidd's portion of said land."
This entry repeats annually through 1862.

[Note: See the section for Benjamin(3) Kidd. This tax list entry suggests a family relationship: this 8 acres is part of the 56 acres owned by Benjamin Kidd, which Ann Kidd is inheriting as his daughter. Ann Kidd then passes the land on to her brother and heir W.S. Kidd , who dies without children, so the land then goes to his brother Richard Kidd and a Dorothy Hart (who may be the daughter of Patsey Kidd who married Thomas Hart). The fact that is particularly interesting is that this 56 acres remains in Benjamin Kidd's estate from 1818 to 1860 for 42 years. In 1860, it is transferred to Ann Kidd, and then by 1863 to the heirs of W.S. Kidd.]

1862 – At a Quarterly Court held for K&Q County on Friday, 7 February 1862, the last will and testament of **Nancy Kidd deceased** was offered for proof and was proved by the oaths of (illegible) Watkins and John B. Dyke, two of the witnesses thereto subscribed.[181]
At a Quarterly Court held for K&Q County on Thursday, 7 August 1862, letters of administration of the estate of **Nancy Kidd**, deceased (with her will annexed) were granted to Jno. B. Dyke, with the oath administered and bond acknowledged.[182],[183] Unfortunately,

---

[180] These are the only records for her that refer to her as Ann Kidd rather than Nancy Kidd. We feel confident that they are one and the same person, because they both indicate that she died in 1862.

[181] King and Queen [County] Minute Book, 1858-1866, page 170, retrieved from FHL #32117, image 209 via familysearch.org. Image available upon request.

[182] King and Queen [County] Minute Book, 1858-1866, page 190, retrieved from FHL #32117, image 228 via familysearch.org. Image available upon request.

[183] *Index to Virginia Estates, 1800-1865*, vol. 10, compiled by Wesley E. Pippenger, published by Virginia Genealogical Society, 2010, citing Minute Book 1858-1866, pp. 170, 190.

this will was evidently lost in the last Courthouse fire; we have been unable to find it. The surviving wills for K&Q date from 1864 and later.

1863 – **Ann Kidd** no longer appears on the K&Q LTL; in 1863 (the last that we've checked), "Richard Kidd and Dorothy Hart" are taxed upon the same land.
[Note: "Nancy Kidd devised by her will her land to W.S. Kidd for life. [infers W.S.] leaving no children, then to Richard Kidd and Dorothy Hart" and "The said W.S. Kidd died leaving no children"]
[Dorothea A. Kidd was born 1827 in K&Q Co to Patsey Kidd and Thomas Hart, married Daniel Holland in Essex Co. on 20 Nov 1862.[184] A Dorotha Hart is on the .1850 federal census in Essex Co, age 23, living in a household headed by Elizabeth Price, along with Maria Price, Richard Robinson, and William Robinson.]

1870 – Dorothy Holland, the same woman as named above, was plaintiff in the following case; the details are not known due to records losses in K&Q:

At a Circuit Court held for K&Q County on Monday 2 May 1870, the case of Dorothy A. Holland, Complainant vs. Jno. B. Dyke, Admr. *de bonis non*[185] with the will annexed of **Nancy Kidd, dec'd**, Defendant was heard.
"The proceedings in this cause (heard?) before W. D. Gresham appointed by the Court under the provisions of an act of the Legislature of Va. on the 21st day of February 1866 a Commissioner to take evidence to establish lost records(,) together with his report, thereupon having been returned to Court more than thirty days and no exceptions taken thereto and it appearing to the Court that the evidence (adduced?) establishes the Contents of Nancy Kidd's will. The Court doth order and decree that the proof taken of the Contents of said will shall be admitted to record and shall have full force and effect as the will of **Nancy Kidd**." [186]

NANCY KIDD, a free black female in 1833

1833 – **Nancy Kidd** appears on a list of free Negroes living in K&Q Co (see Appendix Two for the full list), listed on page 8, noted as living "on own land."[187]

NANCY S. KIDD, named in K&Q Co court record in 1835, as plaintiff in a suit against her sisters Polly Kidd Brown and Harriett Kidd Walton.

---

[184] Virginia, Select Marriages, 1785-1940 on ancestry.com.

[185] Administrator *de bonis non* is a legal term pertaining to assets of an estate following the death or removal of the first administrator of an estate. The second administrator is called the administrator *de bonis non* and distributes the remaining assets. In this case, something caused the executor named in her will to be unable to complete the task, and John B. Dyke was evidently appointed administrator de bonis non. Now, Dorothy Holland, the granddaughter of Nancy Kidd, is suing Dyke over the estate.

[186] K&Q Circuit Court Chancery Orders, 1859-1874, pp. 242-243, retrieved from FHL #32216, images 271-272, via familysearch.org (unrestricted access).

[187] Ibid..

1835 – In a Court held for K&Q Co on 4 November 1835:[188]
> **Nancy S. Kidd,**[189] Plt vs. Thos. F. Spencer in his own right and as Admr. of Thomas Spencer & also as Admr. of John Spencer; Francis Row, Sheriff of K&Q County & (illegible) Admr of Meacham Spencer; Elvin Brown & **Polly his wife who was Polly Kidd** and Isaac Wharton [Walton] & **Harriett his wife who was Harriett Kidd**, Defts.
>
> The Defts **Elvin Browne and Polly his wife** who are now residents of this state and against whom the Plt appears to have provided(?) in the mode proscribed by Law against absent defendants still failing to appear and answer, and it appearing that the subpoena in this cause has been served more than four months upon the Defts **Isaac Walton**[190] **& Harriet his wife** & they still failing to appear and answer the Bill is taken for Confessed as to them & thereupon this Cause coming on to be heard upon the Bill, answer of the defendant Thomas F. Spencer and the exhibit was argued by Counsel upon consideration whereof & the Plt. waiving at this time any claim to a Decree for any part of Mecham Spencer's proportion of the said balance of $934.92 but without prejudice to its apertion(?) hereafter by Consent of parties it is adjudged, ordered and decreed that the defendant Thos. F. Spencer admr. of John Spencer out of the assets of the said John Spencer in his hands, if so much he have, if not out of his own proper goods & chattels pay to the plaintiff Nancy S. Kidd the sum of $101.87 with interest thereon at the rate of six per centum per annum from the 1st day of January 1827 until paid and her costs expended in the prosecution of this suit upon the said **Nancy S. Kidd** or some person for his(?) executing to the said Thomas F. Spencer, admr. of John Spencer a refunding bond with good security conditioned(?) according to Law. But this decree is without prejudice to any claim which the aid Plaintiff may hereafter assert to a proportion of Mecham Spencer's part of the estate of John Spencer or to any claim which the Defts. **Elvin Brown & Polly his wife and Isaac Walton & Harriett his wife** may assert to their portions of John or Mecham Spencer's Estate.

PETER KIDD (b ca 1837), a free Black woodcutter

1853-1854 – A free Negro named "Peter Lee, alias Peter Kidd" appears on the PPTLs for K&Q in these two years:

1853	Peter Lee, alias Peter Kidd	"free Negro"	"FN bet.16-21 yrs old"
1854	Peter Lee, alias Peter Kidd	"free Negro"	"FN bet.16-21 yrs old"

He does not appear on the 1855 PPTL for K&Q; two other free Negroes (Sam/Sam and Billy) do appear on this list. We have not examined subsequent PPTLs for K&Q.

---

[188] Circuit Superior Court of Law and Chancery, Order Books: Order Book, 1831-1851,pp. 52-53, retrieved from LoV ILL reel 2, FHL #32114 unrestricted access, images 71-72. Digital images available upon request.

[189] At this time the identity of this woman is unknown. Note that Benjamin Kidd's first wife was an Ann Spencer. There is only one other mention of Spencer in this BD, in which John(1) Kidd was an adjoining neighbor. – RK

[190] The name is indeed written WHARTON in the title, but WALTON in the body of the record.)

1860 – **Peter Kidd**, age 23, appears on the federal census in K&Q, Centerville and Little Plymouth PO, p 513, with Rachel, age 30 (dwelling and HH number 729). His occupation is given as wood cutter; his personal estate is valued at $29.

PINKEY KIDD, a free black female in 1833

POLLY KIDD(s), two free black females in 1833

1833 – **Pinkey Kidd** and two **Polly Kidds** appear on a list of free black individuals living in K&Q Co (see Appendix Two for the full list). Pinkey Kidd is listed on page 8, noted as living "on own land."   One Polly Kidd also is listed on page 8, noted as living "on own land."[191] The second Polly Kidd is listed below.

POLLY KIDD (ca 1800 - ??), a free Black woman head of household

1813 – A **Polly Kidd** was one of thirteen free Negro household heads with the surname of Kidd who appeared on the K&Q PPTLs for the first time in 1813. While other free Negroes are found on subsequent PPTLs in K&Q, she does not appear again on these annual lists.

1830 – **Polly Kidd** appears on the federal census for K&Q Co as head of a free black household, p 307:

Kidd, Polly (misindexed as Kedd at Ancestry.com), all in HH listed as "free colored persons": 1M 10-23, 2 F under 10, 2 F 10-23, 1 F 36-54, total 6

She is listed next to Samuel Kidd, Hannah Kidd, and Sally Kidd, all free black heads of households in 1830.

1833 – **Polly Kidd** appears on a list of free black individuals living in K&Q Co (see Appendix Two for the full list), listed on page 6, her occupation is given as spinner, noted as living at New Church. Other free Negroes listed as living at New Church were John Kidd, a farmer, William Kidd, a wood cutter, and Sally Kidd, a farmer.[192]

1850 – **Polly Kidd**, a free black woman head of household, appears on the federal census in K&Q Co, Stratton Major Parish, p 180B (dwelling 531 and HH 531), living among both black and white neighbors:
Kidd, Polly [misindexed as Kadd] 50 FB VA no occupation listed
  " , Milly Ann 5 FB VA
  " , John 4 MB VA
  " , Eliza 24 FB VA no occupation listed
  " , George 3 MB VA

1860 – **Polly Kidd**, a free black woman head of household, again appears on the federal census in K&Q Co, Little Plymouth PO, p 517 (dwelling 761 and HH 761), living among black and white neighbors:

---

[191] Ibid.

[192] Virginia. Auditor of Public Accounts (1776-1928). Free blacks records, 1833-1863. APA 757 1082990_0007_0004_0001_0011 Library of Virginia. This information can be found at "Virginia Untold: The African American Narrative," http://www.virginiamemory.com/collections/aan/.

>   **Kidd, Polly** 60 FB weaver $27 (personal estate value) VA
>   "   , Milly Ann 18 FB no occupation listed VA

POLLY KIDD BROWN, the sister of Nancy S. Kidd and Harriet Kidd Walton, and wife of Elvin Brown. She may not have lived in K&Q.

1835 – In a Court held for K&Q Co on 4 November 1835:[193]
> **Nancy S. Kidd,**[194] Plt vs. Thos. F. Spencer in his own right and as Admr. of Thomas Spencer & also as Admr. of John Spencer; Francis Row, Sheriff of K&Q County & (illegible) Admr of Meacham Spencer; Elvin Brown & **Polly his wife who was Polly Kidd** and Isaac Wharton [Walton] & **Harriett his wife who was Harriett Kidd**, Defts.
>
> The Defts **Elvin Browne and Polly his wife** who are now residents of this state and against whom the Plt appears to have provided(?) in the mode proscribed by Law against absent defendants still failing to appear and answer, and it appearing that the subpoena in this cause has been served more than four months upon the Defts **Isaac Walton**[195] **& Harriet his wife** & they still failing to appear and answer the Bill is taken for Confessed as to them & thereupon this Cause coming on to be heard upon the Bill, answer of the defendant Thomas F. Spencer and the exhibit was argued by Counsel upon consideration whereof & the Plt. waiving at this time any claim to a Decree for any part of Mecham Spencer's proportion of the said balance of $934.92 but without prejudice to its apertion(?) hereafter by Consent of parties it is adjudged, ordered and decreed that the defendant Thos. F. Spencer admr. of John Spencer out of the assets of the said John Spencer in his hands, if so much he have, if not out of his own proper goods & chattels pay to the plaintiff Nancy S. Kidd the sum of $101.87 with interest thereon at the rate of six per centum per annum from the 1st day of January 1827 until paid and her costs expended in the prosecution of this suit upon the said **Nancy S. Kidd** or some person for his(?) executing to the said Thomas F. Spencer, admr. of John Spencer a refunding bond with good security conditioned(?) according to Law. But this decree is without prejudice to any claim which the aid Plaintiff may hereafter assert to a proportion of Mecham Spencer's part of the estate of John Spencer or to any claim which the Defts. **Elvin Brown & Polly his wife and Isaac Walton & Harriett his wife** may assert to their portions of John or Mecham Spencer's Estate.

RICHARD KIDD, son of Benjamin (3) and Nancy Kidd, and brother of Benjamin F., Nancy (Ann), William S., and likely Patsey (who married Thomas Hart)
Born ca 1815
Not found in K&Q after 1852

1838-1852 – a **Richard Kidd** first appears on the K&Q PPTLs in 1838. He then appears annually through 1852. Each year he's charged for one white tithe.

1840 – **Richard Kidd** is likely one of the adult males in Nancy Kidd's household on the 1840 federal census in K&Q Co, p. 101. This Nancy Kidd, age 30-39, appears to be his sister

---

[193] Circuit Superior Court of Law and Chancery, Order Books: Order Book, 1831-1851, LoV ILL reel 2, FHL #32114 – restricted access. Pp. 52-53. Digital images available upon request.

[194] At this time the identity of this woman is unknown. Note that Benjamin Kidd's first wife was an Ann Spencer. There is only one other mention of Spencer in this BD, in which John(1) Kidd was an adjoining neighbor. – RK

[195] The name is indeed written WHARTON in the title, but WALTON in the body of the record.)

Nancy, rather than his mother:

Nancy Kidd 1M 5-9, **2 20-29**; 1F 30-39. One free Negro male 10-23 and two slaves (a male less than 10 and a female, 36-54). Three in agriculture. The adult whites could not read or write (no other Kidds on this page or nearby).

1850 – on the federal census in K&Q Co, St. Stephen's Parish, p. 161A, HH 197:
Kidd, Richard 35MW farmer $400 VA
   " , Nancy 67FW   VA
   " , Nancy 42FW   VA
   " , William 17MW laborer VA

The 1850 K&Q Co census slave schedule for **Richard Kidd** lists a female aged 27 and a female aged 10.

1853-1854 – Nancy Kidd appears on the K&Q PPTLs in 1853, the year that **Richard Kidd** drops from the lists, with one white male tithe in her household (this likely would be the William, above). She has no white tithe listed in 1854. In 1855, her estate is listed in the K&Q PPTLs.

It is possible the Richard Kidd who appears in Henrico Co VA in 1860 is this Richard Kidd. However, no Richard appears on the Henrico Co PPTLs.

1860 – A **Richard Kidd** appears on the federal census in the eastern division of Henrico Co, p. 90, Richmond PO:
Kidd, Richard 38MW farmer $1500/$4000   b. VA CROW[196]
Gathright, Archer 19MW laborer VA

Richard Kidd is also found on the 1860 census slave schedule for Henrico Co in 1860, p. 117, with 5 slaves: 2 black females aged 27 and 25, 2 black male children aged 5 and 3, and 1 black female child aged 11 months.

RICHARD KID(D), a free Black farmer

1856 – On 26 December 1856, **Richard Kidd** (age 21, single, born in K&Q, son of John and Jane Kidd, occupation farmer) married Huroutha Lockley (age 16, single, born in K&Q, daughter of John and Mary Wyatt) were married in K&Q by Isaac Diggs, M.G.[197] This abstract did not state the race of the bride or the groom but this is the same couple enumerated on the 1860 census, below.

1860 – **Richard Kid**, age 21, black, a farmer, appears on the federal census in Little Plymouth PO, K&Q Co, p 480, with Henrietta, age 18, mulatto, and Francis A., 3, black female (dwelling and family number 450). His personal estate was valued at $40.

SALLY KIDD, a free black head of household (see also Sarah Kidd, below)

---

[196] Cannot read or write.

[197] *King and Queen County, Virginia Marriage Records. Transcripts of consents, affidavits, minister returns, and marriage licenses, Vol. 1, 1853-1874*, by Suzanne P. Derieux and Wesley E. Pippenger, Tappahannock, Virginia, 2013, page 30, citing "Auditor of Public Accounts copy of the Marriage Register", Library of Virginia, page 5. These marriage registers have been microfilmed by the Library of Virginia. See https://www.lva.virginia.gov/public/guides/BMDregisters/index.htm .

1813 – A **Sally Kidd** was one of thirteen free Negro household heads with the surname of Kidd who appeared on the K&Q PPTLs for the first time in 1813. While other free Negroes are found on subsequent PPTLs in K&Q, a Sally Kidd does not appear again on these annual lists.

1830 – **Sally Kidd** (misindexed as Kedd at Ancestry.com) appears on the federal census for K&Q Co as head of a free black household, p 307. However, the enumeration shows 1 free black **male** 55-99 **and 2 female slaves** 10-23.
Given this record, it would appear that Sally was a male, not a female.

This household is listed next to Samuel Kidd, Hannah Kidd, and Polly Kidd, all free black heads of households.

1833 – **Sally Kidd** appears on a list of free black individuals living in K&Q Co (see Appendix Two for the full list), listed on page 6, his/her occupation is given as farmer, noted as living at New Church. Also listed as living at New Church were John Kidd, a farmer, William Kidd, a wood cutter, and Polly Kidd, a spinner.[198]

It is possible that this Sally Kidd was among the slaves of John Kidd (1). We base this upon the K&Q PPTLs for this John Kidd between 1783 and 1786 in the table below. The names of at least six of the slaves of John Kidd (1) on the 1783-1786 PPTLs match those individuals who appear as free Negroes in the 1813 PPTLs, some 30 years later; Frank, Hannah, Humphrey, James, **Sally** (variously listed as Sally, Sall and Sarah) and Sam Kidd appear on both lists. And John's slave named Will *could* be the same individual as the free Negro Billy Kidd on the 1813 PPTL. Moreover, of these, all but James and Hannah were under the age of 16 in 1783-1786. While the gap of 30 years and the fact that there may have been other slaves with these given names must be considered, it is possible that John, his wife Lucy, or one of their heirs freed their slaves. See the Table below:

YEAR	TAXPAYER	WT	B>16	B<16	H	Cattle	COMMENTS
1782	John	1	4	7	3	17	slaves not named
1783	John	1	3	6	4	15	8 others listed by name: Lucy,[199] James, Molley, Hannah, **Sally**, Sam, Frank, & Will; only 3 over 16. "<u>2 White Souls</u>"
1784	John	1	3	5	3	15	8 named slaves: James, Molley, Hannah, >16; Humphrey, **Sall**, Frank, Tom & Will <16.

---

[198] Virginia. Auditor of Public Accounts (1776-1928). Free blacks records, 1833-1863. APA 757 1082990_0007_0004_0001_0011 Library of Virginia. This information can be found at "Virginia Untold: The African American Narrative," http://www.virginiamemory.com/collections/aan/.

[199] This particular entry is perplexing because of a column heading - # of White Souls- that occurs in this single year, and which listed 2 white souls for John Kidd. We know from other records that his wife's given name was Lucy, and we believe that she is the Lucy in this record, and the second white tithe, in addition to John.

1785	John	1	3	5	3	17	Slaves James, Milly, Hannah, Humphrey, **Sarah**, Peter, Frank & Sam
1786	John	1	4	5	2	16	Slaves James, Humphrey, Hannah, Milly, Peter, **Sary**, Frank, Sam, Will
1787	John	1	5	4	2	15	slaves not named in 1787

SAMUEL KIDD, a free Black farmer

1813-1855 – A free Negro named **Samuel/Sam Kidd** appears almost annually on the PPTLs for
K&Q during this span of 42 years (see Table below):

YEAR	TAXPAYER	NOTATION
1813	Sam Kidd	"free Negro"
1814	Sam Kidd	"free Negro"
1816	Sam Kidd	"free Negro"
1818	Sam Kidd	"free Negro"
1820	Sam Kidd	"free Negro"
1824	Sam Kidd	"free Negro"
1825	Sam Kidd	free Negro
1826	Sam Kidd	"free Negro"
1838[200]	Sam Kidd	"free Negro"
1839	Sam Kidd	"free Negro"
1840	Sam Kidd	"free Negro"
1841	Sam Kidd	"free Negro"
1842	Sam Kidd	"free Negro"
1843	Sam Kidd	"free Negro"
1846	Sam Kidd	"free Negro"
1848	Sam Kidd	"free Negro"
1849	Sam Kidd	"free Negro"
1850	Sam Kidd	"free Negro"

---

[200] Between 1827 and 1835, only ONE free Negro appears on the PPTLs in K&Q; a John Kidd, in 1833. We suspect
that this is due to either the loss of records, or a change in the methodology used by the tax commissioner in these
years, and not the death or departure of these individuals.

1851	Samuel Kidd	"free Negro"
1852	Samuel Kidd	"free Negro"
1853	Sam Kidd	"free Negro"
1854	Sam Kidd	"free Negro"
1855	Samuel Kidd	"free Negro"

Moses and Sam Kidd were listed frequently on the K&Q PPTLs with the white taxpayers (as opposed to appearing on separate lists of free Negroes), whereas the other free Negroes were more often listed only on a separate list for that year. The reason for this (if there is one) is not clear to us.

1820 – on the federal census in K&Q Co listed as **Samuel Kidd,fn (for Free Negro)** with 1 free black male under 14, 1 14-25 and 1 26-44; 3 free black females under 14, 2 14-25, 1 26-44, & 3 45 or over – 12 total, 2 in agriculture.

1830 – **Saml. Kidd** (misindexed as Kedd at Ancestry.com) appears on the federal census for K&Q Co as head of a free black household, p 307:
Saml. Kedd: 2 free males under 10 & **1 free male 36-54**; 5 free females under 10, 2 free females 10-23, 1 free female 24-35, Total all "free colored persons": 11.

This household is listed next to Sally Kidd, Hannah Kidd, and Polly Kidd, all free Black heads of households in 1830.

1833 – **Sam Kidd** appears on a list of free Black individuals living in K&Q Co (see Appendix Two for the full list), listed on page 8, his occupation is given as farmer, and is noted as living "on own land."[201]

1840 – **Samuel Kidd** appears on the federal census in K&Q Co (misindexed as Kedd at Ancestry.com), with 4 free black males under 10, 2 10-23, and 1 55-90; 5 free black females under 10, 4 10-23, 1 24-35, & 1 36-54. Total 18, 7 in agriculture and 1 in mfg and trade.

1850 – We have not been able to find him on the 1850 federal census in K&Q, although he appears on the PPTLs through 1855.

It is possible that this Samuel Kidd was among the slaves of John Kidd (1). We base this upon the K&Q PPTLs for this John Kidd between 1783 and 1786 in the table below. The names of at least six of the slaves of John Kidd (1) on the 1783-1786 PPTLs match those individuals who appear as free Negroes in the 1813 PPTLs, some 30 years later; Frank, Hannah, Humphrey, James, Sally (variously listed as Sally, Sall and Sarah) and **Sam Kidd** appear on both lists. And John's slave named Will *could* be the same individual as the free Negro Billy Kidd on the 1813 PPTL. Moreover, of these, all but James and Hannah were under the age of 16 in 1783-1786. While the gap of 30 years and the fact that there may have been other slaves with these given names must be considered, it is possible that John, his wife Lucy, or one of their heirs freed their slaves.

---

[201] Virginia. Auditor of Public Accounts (1776-1928). Free blacks records, 1833-1863. APA 757 1082990_0007_0004_0001_0011 Library of Virginia. This information can be found at "Virginia Untold: The African American Narrative," http://www.virginiamemory.com/collections/aan/.

YEAR	TAXPAYER	WT	B>16	B<16	H	Cattle	COMMENTS
1782	John	1	4	7	3	17	slaves not named
1783	John	1	3	6	4	15	8 others listed by name: Lucy,[202] James, Molley, Hannah, Sally, **Sam**, Frank, & Will; only 3 over 16. "2 White Souls"
1784	John	1	3	5	3	15	8 named slaves: James, Molley, Hannah, >16; Humphrey, Sall, Frank, Tom & Will <16.
1785	John	1	3	5	3	17	Slaves James, Milly, Hannah, Humphrey, Sarah, Peter, Frank & **Sam**
1786	John	1	4	5	2	16	Slaves James, Humphrey, Hannah, Milly, Peter, Sary, Frank, **Sam**, Will
1787	John	1	5	4	2	15	slaves not named in 1787

SARAH KIDD, a free black female in 1833 (see also Sally Kidd)

1833 – **Sarah Kidd** appears on a list of free black individuals living in K&Q Co (see Appendix Two for the full list), listed on page 6, along with Maria, Polly, Elizabeth, and James Kidd, noted as living on Paul Philpot's land. This may indicate they were a family in the same household.[203]

THOMAS KIDD, War of 1812 soldier

1813-1814 – Sergeant **Thomas Kidd** served in Captain William Hutchason's Infantry [9th V.M., Boyd's] from 7 Apr 1813 to 17 Apr 1813, listed as present 25 Jan 1813, the note on the pay roll in "in council". Thomas also served from 6 Aug 1814 to 19 Sep 1814, present 19 Sep 1814 at Camp Alexander Field near Georgetown. Remark on pay roll is that "it will take officers and soldiers from this 9th Regt from this time to the 26 of this month to reach their respective homes-Sept. 20, 1814".

Ensign **Thomas Kidd** served in Captain William H. Hutchason's Company [9th V.M., Muse's] called into service by Lt. Colonel Elliott Muse of 109th V.M. from 2 Dec 1814 to 10 Dec 1814, present 10 Dec 1814 at King and Queens Court House. Remarks stated "1

---

[202] This particular entry is perplexing because of a column heading - # of White Souls- that occurs in this single year, and which listed 2 white souls for John Kidd. We know from other records that his wife's given name was Lucy, and we believe that she is the Lucy in this record, and the second white tithe, in addition to John.

[203] Ibid.

servant used by the Sgt and Ensign, private property".

There were two enclosures, one was a Subsistence account the other a pay account. Subsistence account included nine days of service from 2 Dec 1814 to 10 Dec 1814, three rations per day, for a total of 27 rations at a cost of twenty cents each for a total of $5.40, due at Middlesex County. Thomas did not use those rations so he was entitled to compensation, along with pay of $5.80 for a total of $11.20, which he received on 1 Oct 1815. [204], [205]

Ensign **Thomas Kidd** was on the muster roll of Captain William Hutcherson's Company from the 9th Regiment, Virginia Militia, commanded by LT. Col. William Boyd from the 7th to the 17th of April 1813 and from the 2nd to the 10th of December 1814. Time of service was 19 days.
Also listed in this Company is John Kidd. [206]

THOMAS KIDD, son of John Kidd(3)

1820-1826 – a **Thomas Kidd** first appears on the K&Q PPTLs in 1820, charged with one white male tithe. Thomas isn't listed in 1821, but then appears annually, 1822 through 1826, when he drops from these tax lists. This is no doubt Thomas, son of John Kidd(3), as the following account shows:

1821 – John Kidd pays taxes on his **son Tom's** account, as recorded in a King & Queen County Sheriff's Account Book, 1821:

John Kidd	
Tax on 277 Acres Land	3.00
47 do belonging to **son Tom**	.51
13 negroes	6.89
6 horses 81¢. 2 gigs $1	1.81
10 County and poor rates	6.30
~~ m fine~~	~~.75~~ (entry written, then crossed out)
	$18.51
To amt brt up	19.26
1820	
tax on 1 County and poor rates	
for William Kidd	1.05
By Poor Order	8.00
	18.51
By Cash	10.51

---

[204]Thomas Kidd CMSR War of 1812, card numbers 38773929, 3990, 4051, 4119, 4188, 4220, original at NAB, viewed 12-30-2009, copies on file.

[205] *Kidds from Virginia Serving in Wartime, 1800-1848*, by William R. Kidd, (self-published), p. 14..

[206] "A Guide to Virginia Militia Units in the War of 1812", by Stuart Lee Butler, pages 468-469, located at LVA, viewed 7-17-2009, WRK.

$18.51[207]

1823-1828 – No **Thomas Kidd** appears under his own name on the K&Q Land Tax Lists. However, in starting in 1823, the LTLs list the John Kidd living on the Mattapony River in the northern part of the county (John Kidd (4) of Lumpkin & Co) as having added 47 acres adjoining his land, and this addition is designated, **"of Thos. Kidd."** This notation continues until 1828.

THOMAS KIDD, of Middlesex Co VA, son of James and Mary Kidd of Urbanna VA

1826 – A survey of land belonging to **Thomas Kidd, deceased**, was carried out 26 April 1826 in K&Q County. The survey shows that the tract contained 81.25 acres lying in <u>MSX County</u>, and "belonging to the estate of Thomas Kidd, dec'd. and sold to James Crittenden." Neighbors to this parcel included Jane Crittenden, the road leading from the New Dragon[208] Bridge, William Kidd and James Stamper. It is not known why this survey was recorded in K&Q Co, unless it is because this tract bordered K&Q Co.[209]

<u>WALKER KIDD</u> – son of William Kidd Sr. of Caroline Co VA
Walker5 (William4, Daniel3, Thomas2, Thomas1) Kidd
Born abt. 1790 in Caroline County[210]
Married Patsy C. Price in Lexington, Fayette Co KY.
Died after the 1840 federal census and before July 1842 in Fayette Co., KY.
(See his entries in the Caroline County, Virginia document)

1808 – On 5 October 1808, a John Kidd and **Walker Kidd** were witnesses to the will of Edwin Motley in K&Q County, Virginia.[211] Edwin Motley was the husband of Elizabeth Kidd, the elder sister of John and **Walker Kidd**.

---

[207] In the article, "King and Queen Sheriff's Account Book, 1821 (continued)," by Susan B. Chiarello, *Magazine of Virginia Genealogy*, volume 51, page 255. Scanned images in the K&Q Source Documents folder.

[208] Dragon Swamp, also known as Dragon Run, is a brackish water tidal/nontidal stream that forms the headwaters of the Piankatank River. Fed by underground springs, surface runoff and numerous feeder swamps, it courses forty miles through the counties of Essex, K&Q, Middlesex and Gloucester. Its main channel serves as the boundary between Essex and Middlesex to the north, and K&Q and Gloucester to the south. See http://www.virginiaplaces.org/watersheds/dragonrun.html for more information.

[209] K&Q Co. Land Plat Book, 1822-1881, LoV reel 21, page 18, reviewed and retrieved by RK July 2018. Scanned images available upon request.

[210] His year of birth is really difficult to estimate. He was a minor (under 21 years of age) in 1802, when his father's will was proved in Court (so born after 1781).
It APPEARS that he was still a minor in 1808 – see below) in Caroline Co. If true, he was born after 1787.
However, he first appears on Caroline Co. PPTLs in 1803, making his DOB **prior** to 1787 (unless he appears then because of his father's death, while still a minor; we believe that this was indeed the case, given the other data elements here).
Compounding things further, his three KY census entries (see 1820, 1830 and 1840, below) give conflicting estimates: 1820 – age 26-44, so born bet. 1776-1794; 1830 – age 30-39, so born bet. 1791-1800; and 1840 – age 50-59, so born bet. 1781-1790. Using the "preponderance of evidence" principle, we estimate that he was born about 1790, perhaps on the cusp of the age brackets in the later censuses.

[211] Lost Records Localities Digital Collection, King & Queen County, Motley, Edwin will, 1809. Library of Virginia, Richmond, VA 23219. This will and codicils can be viewed online: Go to www. http://www.virginiamemory.com/collections/lost and search on Motley.

1810 – **Walker Kidd** appears on the K&Q PPTL, charged with one white tithe, for only one year.

We have found no other mentions of Walker Kidd in K&Q County. See his section in the Caroline County document.

WILLIAM KIDD(s)

WILLIAM KIDD, son of Henry Kidd, named in his father's Essex Co VA will written in 1785. When he and his siblings sold his father's land in 1794, he was listed as of King and Queen Co.

1794 – In an **Essex Co**. deed dated: 15 Dec 1794[212]
        Grantors: John Kidd and Lucy his wife]
            William Kidd   ] of **King and Queen County**

         John Brown and Mary his wife]
         Benjamin Kidd and Sarah his wife]   of Caroline County
         Grantee: Thomas Roane of Essex County
         Consideration: 400 Pounds and one shilling current money
Tract: A Parcel of land in County of Essex and Parish of South Farnham containing 275 acres. Metes and bounds description, mostly referencing distances to certain trees, but did name lines of Haile, Allen and Dix. Included two tracts of land, one containing 124 ½ acres the second 151 acres. Referenced them as "being those tracts of land whereon Henry Kidd lately lived and of which he died seized and which the said John and **William Kidd**, Mary Brown and Sarah Kidd are entitled to under the last will and testament of the said Henry Kidd."

        Signed and sealed: Jno Kidd
              William Kidd
              John Brown
              Benjamin Kidd
    Witnesses: William Wood
              John Allen
              Philemon Purkins
              James Allen
    Deed rec.: 15 Dec 1794

WILLIAM KIDD(s) UNPLACED

WILLIAM KIDD – 1780s in K&Q Co

1784 – a **William Kidd** appears on the K&Q PPTL for this year, charged with one white male tithe. He then disappears from the PPTLs of K&Q.

---

[212] Essex County (VA) Deed Book 34, p. 91 (also pp 205, 206 and 207), John Kidd et al to Thomas Roane, Abstracted by Nancy Heuser for Sandra Kidd, Oct. 2007. Note: "The deed then had a "p.s. Two graveyards excepted with half an acre of land around the one where the white people are buried and the privilege of carrying any corps to the same."
Pgs. 205, 207 and 207 are the relinquishments of dower by the three women, Lucy Kidd, Mary Brown and Sarah Kidd [the latter the wife of Benjamin Kidd].

Also appearing on the tax list for this year is "Henry Kidd's property" (consisting of an overseer and 4 taxable male slaves). See Henry Kidd's section of this compilation.

1788 – the records of the Upper K&Q Baptist Church in 1788, abstracted in the Virginia Genealogical Society Quarterly, include the following:
"**William Kidd, Sr.**, dec'd, **William Kidd, Jr**, dead." Other Kidd individuals mentioned in these church records are Fanny Kidd, Molley Kidd, Edmund Kidd and John Kidd. [213] [Note: The preface to the abstract of this record states, "The notations after the names were obviously penned at later dates, which may mean these two men named William Kidd died at a date later than 1788."]

WILLIAM KIDD – on K&Q Co 1806-1807 and 1820-1821 tax lists

1806-1807 – a **William Kidd** appears on the K&Q PPTL in these years, charged with one white male tithe. He then disappears from the tax list.

1820-1821 – a **William Kidd** appears on the K&Q PPTLs, charged with one white male tithe, for one year. This may be the same William Kidd listed below:

WILLIAM KIDD, named in 1820 account of John Kidd (3), relationship not known

1821 -- John Kidd pays taxes on his son Tom's account, and an 1820 tax for **William Kidd**, as recorded in a King & Queen County Sheriff's Account Book, 1821:

John Kidd

Tax on 277 Acres Land	3.00
47 do belonging to **son Tom**	.51
13 negroes	6.89
6 horses 81¢. 2 gigs $1	1.81
10 County and poor rates	6.30
~~m fine~~	~~.75~~
	$18.51
To amt brt up	19.26
1820	
tax on 1 County and poor rates for **William Kidd**	1.05
By Poor Order	8.00
	18.51
By Cash	10.51
	$18.51[214]

WILLIAM KIDD, a free black wood cutter in 1833

1833 – **William Kidd** appears on a list of free black individuals living in K&Q Co (see Appendix Two for the full list), listed on page 6, his occupation is given as wood cutter, noted as living

---

[213] *Upper King and Queen Baptist Church Records, King and Queen County, 1774-1788*, transcribed by Richard Slatten and Edgar MacDonald, published in Virginia Genealogical Society *Quarterly*, vol. 30, no. 1, p. 64, February 1992.

[214] In the article, "King and Queen Sheriff's Account Book, 1821 (continued)," by Susan B. Chiarello, *Magazine of Virginia Genealogy*, volume 51, page 255. Scanned images in the K&Q Source Documents folder.

at New Church. Also listed as living at New Church were John Kidd, a farmer, Sally Kidd, a farmer, and Polly Kidd, a spinner.[215]

WILLIAM KIDD (b ca 1815--), a free black tradesman (perhaps the same as the William Kidd, woodcutter, above)

1840 – there is a free black male named **Wm. Kidd**, age 10-23 and living alone, on the federal census in K&Q Co. He's listed as in "Mfg. & trade."

1850 – **William Kidd**, a free black laborer, aged 35, appears on the 1850 census in Stratton Major Parish, K&Q Co, p 164B, with Henrietta Wyatt, aged 13, in his household (dwelling and HH 261).

This same **William Kidd** appears on the Stratton Major Parish, K&Q Co, 1850 census slave schedule, with one black female slave, aged 35. We know it is the same William Kidd because his neighbors are the same on both the 1850 census and the slave schedule.

WILLIAM S. (W.S.) KIDD, the son of Benjamin(3) and Nancy Kidd and brother of Benjamin F., Richard, Nancy (Ann), and likely Patsey (who married Thomas Hart) Born abt 1833 in K&Q County, Virginia Died by 1863 without heirs

1850 – on federal census in K&Q Co, St. Stephen's Parish, p. 161A, HH 197:
Kidd, Richard 35MW farmer $400 VA
  " , Nancy 67FW   VA
  " , Nancy 42FW VA
  " , **William** 17MW laborer VA
On this census, William (S.) Kidd is living in his older brother Richard's household, along with their mother Nancy (1) and their sister Nancy (2).

1860 – on federal census in K&Q Co, Carlton's Store P.O., p. 74, HH 601:
Kidd, William 26MW day laborer $50/$25 VA cannot read or write
HH 602
Kidd, Nancy 50FW weaver $300/$170 VA cannot read or write
(nearby, HH 605 is a John H. Thurston, who was a neighbor of Benjamin Kidd)

[Note: this William is the W.S. Kidd who died by 1863 without heirs, whose inheritance of 8 acres from his sister Nancy's will then goes to his brother Richard Kidd and his niece Dorothy Hart. See the sections for Benjamin Kidd and Nancy Kidd (2).]

---

[215] Virginia. Auditor of Public Accounts (1776-1928). Free blacks records, 1833-1863. APA 757 1082990_0007_0004_0001_0011 Library of Virginia. This information can be found at "Virginia Untold: The African American Narrative," http://www.virginiamemory.com/collections/aan/.

APPENDIX ONE: SOURCES USED IN THE CREATION OF THIS COMPILATION

The following sources of genealogical and historical information on King & Queen County have been identified, using the web sites for the LDS library, the Library of Virginia, and WorldCat. **Each of them has been reviewed and abstracted**, and all Kidd entries in them have been added to this compilation.

PRIMARY SOURCES

1. U.S. Federal censuses, 1810-1850.

2. King & Queen County Personal Property Tax Lists (PPTLs), 1782-1855 (LDS microfilms #32121, 32122 and 32123, reviewed and abstracted by RK)

3. King & Queen County Land Tax Lists, 1782-1863, reviewed and abstracted by SKK.

4. King & Queen County Chancery Court cases, 1804-1913, Library of Virginia website (prior to 1860).

5. Circuit Superior Court of Law and Chancery, Order Books:
Order Book, 1831-1851, index, 615 pp. (LoV ILL reel 2) & FHL #32114 – restricted access
Order Book, 1831-1843, index, pp. 1-377 (LoV ILL reel 8) & FHL #1986818, item 5 – restricted access.
Chancery Order Book, 1831-1858, index, 596 pages (LoV ILL reel 3) – reviewed by RK July 2018

6. K&Q Land Plat Book, 1822-1881, index, 92 pp. (LoV ILL reel 21) – reviewed by RK July 2018

7. Virginia Lost Records Digital Collection, 1674-1894, viewable online at www.virginiamemory.com/collections/lost [one item for K&Q: the 1838 will of Ann Kidd recorded in Chancery Court causes].

8. Ellen Gertrude Tompkins Kidd papers, 1791-1998. Accession number 52005. Personal papers collection, Library of Virginia, Richmond, VA; viewed by RK July 2018. A summary of these records and an inventory of them are available on the LoV website, under Archives & Manuscripts.

SECONDARY SOURCES (arranged alphabetically by **author**) (each has been examined and all Kidd entries in them have been added to this compilation):

1. *Virginia Revolutionary Claims*, compiled and transcribed by Janice L. **Abercrombie** and Richard Slatten, Iberian Publishing Co., Athens, GA, 1992 (three volumes in 1, 1113 pages).

2. *King and Queen County, Virginia*, by Rev. Alfred **Bagby**, Regional Publishing Co., Baltimore, MD, 1973. (The original book was published in 1908.) This book is available online in the catalog at Familysearch.org and Ancestry.com.

3. *The Vestry Book of Stratton Major Parish, King and Queen County, Virginia, 1729-1783*, by C.G. **Chamberlayne**, Stratton Major Parish (Va.), Division of Purchase and Printing, 1931.

4. *A True Relation of the History of King and Queen County in Virginia, 1607-1790*, by Edwin **Cox**, 21 pp., 1976.

5. *King and Queen County, Virginia Marriage Records. Transcripts of consents, affidavits, minister returns, and marriage licenses, Vol. 1, 1853-1874*, by Suzanne P. **Derieux** and Wesley E. Pippenger, Tappahannock, Virginia, 2013.

6. *King and Queen County, Virginia Marriage Records. Transcripts of consents, affidavits, minister returns, and marriage licenses, Vol. 2, 1875-1886,* by Suzanne P. **Derieux** and Wesley E. Pippenger, Tappahannock, Virginia, 2013.

7. *Vital Records of Three Burned Counties: Births, Marriages, and Deaths of King & Queen, King William and New Kent Counties, Virginia, 1680-1860,* by Theresa **Fisher**, Heritage Books, 1998.

8. *Virginia Colonial Abstracts,* Vol. II, Records Concerning 18th Century Persons, 1st through 9th collections, abstracted by Beverley **Fleet**.

9. *King and Queen Co. VA marriages and deaths (1736-1982),* (extracted from the **Henley** marriage/obituary index – personal name index to more than 51,000 marriage and obituary notices published primarily in Richmond-area newspapers between 1736 and 1982, with an emphasis on the years 1780 to 1910."
Virginia Tidewater genealogy. Newport news, VA. v.38, no.1 (Mar. 2007), p. 25-31.
Only one mention of Kidds (the marriage announcement of John Boulware Kidd and his first wife, Anna Roberta Tompkins).

10. *Land and Heritage in the Virginia Tidewater: a History of King and Queen County,* by Barbara Beigun **Kaplan**, 1993. SPL

11. *Kidd's from Virginia serving in wartime, 1800 to 1848,* Compiled by William R **Kidd**, 2009.s

12. *Index to Virginia Estates, 1800-1865,* vol. 10, King and Queen Co citations, compiled by Wesley E. **Pippenger**, published by Virginia Genealogical Society, 2010.

13. *Upper King and Queen Baptist Church Records, King and Queen County, 1774-1788,* transcribed by Richard **Slatten** and Edgar MacDonald, published in Virginia Genealogical Society *Quarterly*, vol. 30, no. 1, pp. 60-64 , February 1992. Also published by TLC Genealogy, Miami, Florida: TLC Genealogy, 1996, 11 pages. [Note from VGS *Quarterly* preface: "The church was organized on August 17, 1774, from the United Baptist Church of Essex County." All extant records (covering any surviving lists up to 1855) are held by the Library of Virginia and available on microfilm. This article covers the first list, consisting of 11 pages.]

14. *Middlesex County, Virginia, deed book 1 (1687-1750) and miscellaneous records (1752-1831),* **T.L.C. Genealogy**, Miami Beach, FL, c1992.
NOTE: "The Miscellaneous Records, which were compiled from loose papers, have much material from the burned record counties of King & Queen and Gloucester."
(RK owns a copy of this book. No records pertaining to Kidds in K&Q in this book.)

15. *Some Marriages in the Burned Record Counties of Virginia,* by the **Virginia Genealogical Society**, 1972.

Although this list is relatively short, it includes all the extant sources that we can find, other than the manuscript and archival collections at the Library of Virginia, which we have not been able to search. Such is the extent of record loss for King & Queen County.

APPENDIX TWO: FREE BLACKS IN KING & QUEEN COUNTY, MARCH 1833

On 4 March 1833, an Act of General Assembly was passed "making appropriations for the removal of free persons of color" to the western coast of Africa and established a board of commissioners charged with carrying out the provisions of the act. Localities were required to report to the board regarding their ability to find free blacks who were willing to relocate to Liberia, though many were unable to find people willing to or able to do so. For those localities that identified free blacks, the reports included names, ages, and sometimes height, occupation, or locality.[216] One such list was compiled for King & Queen County.[217] This list names over 300 individuals, including 26 with the surname of Kidd.

A number of these individuals also appear on the K&Q personal property tax lists, identified as Free Negros or FN.

Page	NAME	Gender	Occupation	Place of abode
6	Sally Kidd	F	Farmer	New Church
6	John Kidd	M	Farmer	New Church
6	William Kidd	M	Wood cutting	New Church
6	Polly Kidd	F	Spinner	New Church
6	Maria Kidd	F	-	Paul Philpot's land
6	Sarah Kidd	F	-	Paul Philpot's land
6	Polly Kidd	F	-	Paul Philpot's land
6	Elizabeth Kidd	F	-	Paul Philpot's land
6	James Kidd	M	-	Paul Philpot's land
6	Elizabeth Kidd	F	-	Henry Ware's land
6	Humphrey Kidd	M	Farmer	George Moore's land
7	Hannah Williams	F		Frank KIDD's
8	Moses Kidd	M	Carpenter	Abt Centerville
8	Frank Kidd	M	Farmer	On own land
8	Sam Kidd	M	Farmer	On own land
8	Kitty Kidd	F	Spinner	On own land
8	Polly Kidd	F	-	On own land

---

216 Virginia. Auditor of Public Accounts (1776-1928). Free blacks records, 1833-1863. APA 757 1082990_0007_0004_0001_0011 Library of Virginia. This information can be found at "Virginia Untold: The African American Narrative," http://www.virginiamemory.com/collections/aan/.

Page	NAME	Gender	Occupation	Place of abode
8	Lucy Kidd	F	-	On own land
8	Nancy Kidd	F	-	On own land
8	Frances Kidd	F	-	On own land
8	Louisa Kidd	F	-	On own land
8	Esperella Kidd	F	-	On own land
8	Pinkey Kidd	F	-	On own land
8	Elmira Kidd	F	-	On own land
8	George Kidd	M	-	On own land
8	John Kidd	M	-	On own land

The Library of Virginia has created a list of all free African Americans found on the K&Q PPTLs between 1782 and 1823. See http://www.freeafricanamericans.com/king&q.htm
Recall that part of the reason for the large numbers of 'free blacks' in King and Queen were the interactions and racial confusions with the Mataponi tribe (occurring since the settlement of the area). The tribal members living on the reservation would not be listed because they were not taxed. Their relatives living off the reservation were taxed and most often listed as "mulatto," but also as "F.N." They are almost never classified as "Indian."

Readers interested in researching pre-Civil War Virginia records for African Americans may find the resources below useful:

Digital Collections Search Tips (prepared by the Library of Virginia, May 2018:
http://www.virginiamemory.com/collections/aan/aan_related_resources.pdf

Slavery in Virginia; A Selected Bibliography (a downloadable 12-page bibliography prepared by David Feinberg of the Library of Virginia, February 2007):
https://www.lva.virginia.gov/public/guides/SlaveryInVA.pdf

APPENDIX THREE: FREE NEGROES ON THE K&Q PERSONAL PROPERTY TAX LISTS, 1813-1855

In the process of reviewing the Personal Property Tax Lists (PPTLs) for K&Q from 1782 through 1855 for any Kidd listings,[218] we discovered that numerous free Negroes with the surname of Kidd or Kid appeared at least intermittently on these PPTLs, starting in 1813. In some instances, they were listed on the same tax list as the white taxpayers; in other years, their names were appended to the white PPTLs, in a separate schedule. The listings vary from year to year, with quite a few years in which no Black Kidd individuals appear; in most if not all of these, the same individuals reappear in subsequent PPTLs, suggesting a degree of variability in the diligence of recording free Negroes (or the method for recording them) from year to year.

It is worth noting that we've examined the PPTLs of over 20 Virginia counties, and have never encountered more than a handful of free Negroes in any other county.

The 1813 PPTL for K&Q is particularly interesting. In that year, no fewer than eleven different free Negroes with the surname of Kidd appeared on the PPTL for one of the two tax districts of K&Q. This raises a question that we cannot at present answer, at least without further research: were these individuals recently freed? And if so, by whom?

In this compilation, we have listed each of the free Negroes found in K&Q records in the alphabetical listing of all Kidds in K&Q County, and included each mention of them in chronological order (whether on the PPTLs or in other records). Viewing the accompanying tables (see next page) of all free Negroes with the surname of Kidd in the PPTLs from 1782 to 1855 may help the reader achieve a broader view and infer possible relationships among them.

The Library of Virginia has created a list of all free African Americans on the K&Q PPTLS from 1782-1823: see http://www.freeafricanamericans.com/king&q.htm.

---

[218] These PPTLs have been microfilmed and more recently were digitized by the Family History Library. They are available online via familysearch.org, but access is restricted to viewing at a Family History Center: FHL #32120, PPTLs, 1782-1803; #32121, 1804-1823; #32122, 1824-1846; and #32123, 1847-1855.

TABLE ONE: FREE NEGROES WITH THE SURNAME OF KIDD FOUND ON K&Q PPTLS, 1813-1855, SORTED BY YEAR, THEN NAME

YEAR	LIST	NAME	NOTATION	COMMENTS
1813	A	Humphrey Kidd	"free Negro"	Dist. Of Benj. Faulkner
1813	A	Billy Kidd Jr.	"free Negro"	Dist. Of Benj. Faulkner
1813	A	Ned Kidd	"free Negro"	Dist. Of Benj. Faulkner
1813	A	James Kidd	"free Negro"	Dist. Of Benj. Faulkner
1813	A	Moses Kidd	"free Negro"	Dist. Of Benj. Faulkner
1813	A	Frank Kidd	"free Negro"	Dist. Of Benj. Faulkner
1813	A	Dick Kidd	"free Negro"	Dist. Of Benj. Faulkner
1813	A	Sam Kidd	"free Negro"	Dist. Of Benj. Faulkner
1813	A	Billy Kidd	"free Negro"	Dist. Of Benj. Faulkner
1813	A	Sally Kidd	"free Negro"	Dist. Of Benj. Faulkner
1813	A	Polly Kidd	"free Negro"	Dist. Of Benj. Faulkner
1814	A	Humphrey Kidd	"free Negro"	Dist. Of John W. Fleet
1814	A	James Kidd	"free Negro"	Dist. Of John W. Fleet
1814	A	Frank Kidd	"free Negro"	Dist. Of John W. Fleet
1814	A	Sam Kidd	"free Negro"	Dist. Of John W. Fleet
1814	A	Dick Kidd	"free Negro"	Dist. Of John W. Fleet
1814	A	Moses Kidd	"free Negro"	Dist. Of John W. Fleet
1814	A	Edward Kidd	"free Negro"	Dist. Of John W. Fleet
1814	A	Billy Kidd	"free Negro"	Dist. Of John W. Fleet
1815	A & B	no F. N. listed		
1816	A	Frank Kidd	"free Negro"	Dist. Of Francis Row
1816	A	Moses Kidd	"free Negro"	Dist. Of Francis Row
1816	A	Ned Kidd	"free Negro"	Dist. Of Francis Row
1816	A	Sam Kidd	"free Negro"	Dist. Of Francis Row
1816	A	Billy Kidd	"free Negro"	Dist. Of Francis Row
1816	A	Dick Kidd	"free Negro"	Dist. Of Francis Row
1816	A	Humphrey Kidd	"free Negro"	Dist. Of Francis Row
1816	A	Humphrey Kidd Sr.	"free Negro"	Dist. Of Francis Row
1817	B	Humphrey Kidd	"free Negro"	Dist. Of Francis Row. Only FN listed
1818	B	Frank Kidd	"free Negro"	List of F. Row; separate list at end
1818	B	Humphrey	"free Negro"	List of F. Row; separate list at end

1818	B	James Kidd	"free Negro"	List of F. Row; separate list at end
1818	B	Moses Kidd	"free Negro"	List of F. Row; separate list at end
1818	B	Billy Kidd	"free Negro"	List of F. Row; separate list at end
1818	B	Sam Kidd	"free Negro"	List of F. Row; separate list at end
1818	B	Edward Kidd	"free Negro"	List of F. Row; separate list at end
1819	A	NONE		
1820	A	Moses Kidd	"free Negro"	List of F. Row; separate list at end
1820	A	Humphrey	"free Negro"	List of F. Row; separate list at end
1820	A	Frank Kidd	"free Negro"	List of F. Row; separate list at end
1820	A	James Kidd	"free Negro"	List of F. Row; separate list at end
1820	A	Sam Kidd	"free Negro"	List of F. Row; separate list at end
1820	A	Edward Kidd	"free Negro"	List of F. Row; separate list at end
1821	*	NONE		
1822	*	NONE		
1823	*	NONE		
1824	*	Sam Kidd	"free Negro"	The only FN listed this year
1825	*	Sam Kidd		The only FN listed this year
1826	*	Sam Kidd	"free Negro"	The only FN listed on main list this yr
1826	*	Humphrey Kidd	"free Negro"	On separate list of FN for this year
1826	*	Moses Kidd	"free Negro"	On separate list of FN for this year
1826	*	Frank Kidd	"free Negro"	On separate list of FN for this year
1826	*	James Kidd	"free Negro"	On separate list of FN for this year
1827	*	NONE		57 free Negroes on separate list[219]
1828	*	NONE		
1829	*	NONE		
1830	*	NONE		
1831	*	NONE		
1832	*	NONE		
1833	*	John Kidd	"free Negro"	the single FN on this list
1834	*	NONE		
1835	*	NONE		
1836	*	Moses Kidd	"free Negro"	Only one on this list
1837	*	Moses Kidd	"free Negro"	Only one on this list

---

[219] See http://www.freeafricanamericans.com/king&q.htm for an abstract of the K&Q PPTL listings of free Negroes from 1782 through 1823.

1838	*	James Kidd	"free Negro"	
1838	*	Sam Kidd	"free Negro"	
1838	*	Moses Kidd	"free Negro"	
1839	*	Sam Kidd	"free Negro"	separate schedule after main list
1839	*	Moses Kidd	"free Negro"	separate schedule after main list
1840	*	Sam Kidd	"free Negro"	Listed with W polls
1840	*	Moses Kidd	"free Negro"	Listed with W polls
1840	*	George Kidd	"free Negro"	Listed with W polls
1840	*	James Kidd	"free Negro"	Listed with W polls
1841	*	James Kidd	"free Negro"	Listed with W polls
1841	*	Sam Kidd	"free Negro"	Listed with W polls
1841	*	George Kidd	"free Negro"	Listed with W polls
1841	*	Moses Kidd	"free Negro"	Listed with W polls
1842	*	Moses Kidd	"free Negro"	Listed with W polls
1842	*	Sam Kidd	"free Negro"	Listed with W polls
1842	*	James Kidd	"free Negro"	On separate list at end this year
1842	*	Frank Kidd	"free Negro"	On separate list at end this year
1842	*	Billy Kidd	"free Negro"	On separate list at end this year
1842	*	George Kidd	"free Negro"	On separate list at end this year
1842	*	John Kidd	"free Negro"	On separate list at end this year
1843	*	Moses Kidd	"free Negro"	List of John Pollard, with W polls
1843	*	James Kidd	"free Negro"	On separate list at end this year
1843	*	Sam Kidd	"free Negro"	On separate list at end this year
1843	*	Billy Kidd	"free Negro"	On separate list at end this year
1843	*	George Kidd	"free Negro"	On separate list at end this year
1844	*	Moses Kidd	"free Negro"	with W polls; no separate list
1845	*	Moses Kidd	"free Negro"	with W polls; no separate list
1846	*	Sam Kidd	"free Negro"	with W polls; no separate list
1846	*	Moses Kidd	"free Negro"	with W polls; no separate list
1847	*	Moses Kidd	"free Negro"	with W polls; no separate list
1847	*	Billy Kidd	"free Negro"	with W polls; no separate list
1848	*	Sam Kidd	"free Negro"	with W polls; no separate list
1848	*	Moses Kidd	"free Negro"	with W polls; no separate list
1849	*	Billy Kidd	"free Negro"	with W polls; pays tax for two slaves
1849	*	Sam Kidd	"free Negro"	List of John Pollard; with W polls
1849	*	Moses Kidd	"free Negro"	List of John Pollard; with W polls

1850	*	Billy Kidd	"free Negro"	with W polls; pays tax for two slaves
1850	*	George Kidd	"free Negro"	with W polls
1850	*	Sam Kidd	"free Negro"	with W polls
1851	*	Samuel Kidd	"free Negro"	with W polls
1851	*	William Kidd	"free Negro"	with W polls
1851	*	George Kidd	"free Negro"	with W polls
1852	*	Samuel Kidd	"free Negro"	with W polls
1852	*	William Kidd	"free Negro"	with W polls
1852	*	George Kidd	"free Negro"	with W polls
1853	*	Peter Lee, alias Peter Kidd	"free Negro"	"FN bet.16-21 yrs old"
1853	*	William Kidd	"free Negro"	
1853	*	Sam Kidd	"free Negro"	
1854	*	Peter Lee, alias Peter Kidd	"free Negro"	"FN bet.16-21 yrs old"
1854	*	William Kidd	"free Negro"	
1854	*	Sam Kidd	"free Negro"	
1855	*	Samuel Kidd	"free Negro"	
1855	*	Billy Kidd	"free Negro"	

See the next page for a Table sorted by Name, then by Year.

TABLE TWO: FREE NEGROES WITH THE SURNAME OF KIDD FOUND ON K&Q PPTLS, 1813-1855, SORTED BY NAME, THEN YEAR

YEAR	LIST	NAME	NOTATION	COMMENTS
1813	A	Billy Kidd	"free Negro"	Dist. Of Benj. Faulkner
1813	A	Billy Kidd Jr.	"free Negro"	Dist. Of Benj. Faulkner
1814	A	Billy Kidd	"free Negro"	Dist. of John W. Fleet
1816	A	Billy Kidd	"free Negro"	Dist. Of Francis Row
1818	B	Billy Kidd	"free Negro"	List of F. Row; separate list at end
1842	*	Billy Kidd	"free Negro"	On separate list at end this year
1843	*	Billy Kidd	"free Negro"	On separate list at end this year
1847	*	Billy Kidd	"free Negro"	with W polls; no separate list
1849	*	Billy Kidd	"free Negro"	with W polls; pays tax for two slaves
1850	*	Billy Kidd	"free Negro"	with W polls; pays tax for two slaves
1855	*	Billy Kidd	"free Negro"	
1813	A	Dick Kidd	"free Negro"	Dist. Of Benj. Faulkner
1814	A	Dick Kidd	"free Negro"	Dist. Of John W. Fleet
1816	A	Dick Kidd	"free Negro"	Dist. Of Francis Row
1813	A	Ned Kidd	"free Negro"	Dist. Of Benj. Faulkner
1814	A	Edward Kidd	"free Negro"	Dist. Of John W. Fleet
1816	A	Ned Kidd	"free Negro"	Dist. Of Francis Row
1818	B	Edward Kidd	"free Negro"	List of F. Row; separate list at end
1820	A	Edward Kidd	"free Negro"	List of F. Row; separate list at end
1813	A	Frank Kidd	"free Negro"	Dist. Of Benj. Faulkner
1814	A	Frank Kidd	"free Negro"	Dist. of John W. Fleet
1816	A	Frank Kidd	"free Negro"	Dist. Of Francis Row
1818	B	Frank Kidd	"free Negro"	List of F. Row; separate list at end

1820	A	Frank Kidd	"free Negro"	List of F. Row; separate list at end
1826	*	Frank Kidd	"free Negro"	On separate list of FN
1842	*	Frank Kidd	"free Negro"	On separate list at end
1840	*	George Kidd	"free Negro"	Listed with W polls
1841	*	George Kidd	"free Negro"	Listed with W polls
1842	*	George Kidd	"free Negro"	On separate list at end
1843	*	George Kidd	"free Negro"	On separate list at end
1850	*	George Kidd	"free Negro"	with W polls
1851	*	George Kidd	"free Negro"	with W polls
1852	*	George Kidd	"free Negro"	with W polls
1813	A	Humphrey Kidd	"free Negro"	Dist. Of Benj. Faulkner
1814	A	Humphrey Kidd	"free Negro"	Dist. of John W. Fleet
1816	A	Humphrey Kidd	"free Negro"	Dist. Of Francis Row
1816	A	Humphrey Kidd Sr.	"free Negro"	Dist. Of Francis Row
1817	B	Humphrey Kidd	"free Negro"	Dist. Of Francis Row; only FN listed this year
1818	B	Humphrey Kidd	"free Negro"	List of F. Row; separate list at end
1820	A	Humphrey Kidd	"free Negro"	List of F. Row; separate list at end
1826	*	Humphrey Kidd	"free Negro"	On separate list of FN

1813	A	James Kidd	"free Negro"	Dist. Of Benj. Faulkner
1814	A	James Kidd	"free Negro"	Dist. of John W. Fleet
1818	B	James Kidd	"free Negro"	List of F. Row; separate list at end
1820	A	James Kidd	"free Negro"	List of F. Row; separate list at end
1826	*	James Kidd	"free Negro"	On separate list of FN
1838	*	James Kidd	"free Negro"	
1840	*	James Kidd	"free Negro"	Listed with W polls

1841	*	James Kidd	"free Negro"	Listed with W polls
1842	*	James Kidd	"free Negro"	On separate list at end
1843	*	James Kidd	"free Negro"	On separate list at end
1833	*	John Kidd	"free Negro"	Only FN on this list
1842	*	John Kidd	"free Negro"	On separate list at end
1813	A	Moses Kidd	"free Negro"	Dist. Of Benj. Faulkner
1814	A	Moses Kidd	"free Negro"	Dist. of John W. Fleet
1816	A	Moses Kidd	"free Negro"	Dist. Of Francis Row
1818	B	Moses Kidd	"free Negro"	List of F. Row; separate list at end
1820	A	Moses Kidd	"free Negro"	List of F. Row; separate list at end
1826	*	Moses Kidd	"free Negro"	On separate list of FN
1836	*	Moses Kidd	"free Negro"	Only FN on this list
1837	*	Moses Kidd	"free Negro"	Only FN on this list
1838	*	Moses Kidd	"free Negro"	
1839	*	Moses Kidd	"free Negro"	separate list at end
1840	*	Moses Kidd	"free Negro"	with W polls
1841	*	Moses Kidd	"free Negro"	with W polls
1842	*	Moses Kidd	"free Negro"	with W polls
1843	*	Moses Kidd	"free Negro"	with W polls
1844	*	Moses Kidd	"free Negro"	with W polls
1845	*	Moses Kidd	"free Negro"	with W polls
1846	*	Moses Kidd	"free Negro"	with W polls
1847	*	Moses Kidd	"free Negro"	with W polls
1848	*	Moses Kidd	"free Negro"	with W polls
1849	*	Moses Kidd	"free Negro"	with W polls

1853	*	Peter Lee, alias Peter Kidd	"free Negro"	"FN bet.16-21 yrs old"
1854	*	Peter Lee, alias Peter Kidd	"free Negro"	"FN bet.16-21 yrs old"
1813	A	Polly Kidd	"free Negro"	Dist. Of Benj. Faulkner

1813	A	Sally Kidd	"free Negro"	Dist. Of Benj. Faulkner
1813	A	Sam Kidd	"free Negro"	Dist. Of Benj. Faulkner
1814	A	Sam Kidd	"free Negro"	Dist .of John W. Fleet
1816	A	Sam Kidd	"free Negro"	Dist. Of Francis Row
1818	B	Sam Kidd	"free Negro"	List of F. Row; separate list at end
1820	A	Sam Kidd	"free Negro"	List of F. Row; separate list at end
1824	*	Sam Kidd	"free Negro"	only FN listed
1825	*	Sam Kidd		only FN listed
1826	*	Sam Kidd	"free Negro"	only FN listed on main lis
1838	*	Sam Kidd	"free Negro"	
1839	*	Sam Kidd	"free Negro"	separate list
1840	*	Sam Kidd	"free Negro"	Listed with W polls
1841	*	Sam Kidd	"free Negro"	Listed with W polls
1842	*	Sam Kidd	"free Negro"	Listed with W polls
1843	*	Sam Kidd	"free Negro"	separate list at end
1846	*	Sam Kidd	"free Negro"	with W polls
1848	*	Sam Kidd	"free Negro"	with W polls
1849	*	Sam Kidd	"free Negro"	with W polls
1850	*	Sam Kidd	"free Negro"	with W polls
1851	*	Samuel Kidd	"free Negro"	with W polls
1852	*	Samuel Kidd	"free Negro"	with W polls
1853	*	Sam Kidd	"free Negro"	
1854	*	Sam Kidd	"free Negro"	
1855	*	Samuel Kidd	"free Negro"	
1851	*	William Kidd	"free Negro"	with W polls
1852	*	William Kidd	"free Negro"	with W polls
1853	*	William Kidd	"free Negro"	
1854	*	William Kidd	"free Negro"	

www.ingramcontent.com/pod-product-compliance
Lightning Source LLC
Chambersburg PA
CBHW081619250726
48657CB00009B/2635